GLOBALVIEWPOINTS

Freedom of Expression

Other Books of Related Interest:

Current Controversies Series

Domestic Wiretapping

Homeland Security

Introducing Issues with Opposing Viewpoints Series

The Patriot Act

Issues on Trial

Free Speech

GLOBALVIEWPOINTS

Freedom of Expression

Alicia Cafferty Lerner and Adrienne Wilmoth Lerner,
Book Editors

GREENHAVEN PRESS
A part of Gale, Cengage Learning

GALE
CENGAGE Learning

Detroit • New York • San Francisco • New Haven, Conn • Waterville, Maine • London

Christine Nasso, *Publisher*
Elizabeth Des Chenes, *Managing Editor*

© 2009 Greenhaven Press, a part of Gale, Cengage Learning

LIBRARY OF CONGRESS CATALOGING-IN-PUBLICATION DATA

Freedom of expression / Alicia Cafferty Lerner and Adrienne Wilmoth Lerner, book editors.
    p. cm. -- (Global viewpoints)
    Includes bibliographical references and index.
    ISBN 978-0-7377-4154-4 (hardcover)
    ISBN 978-0-7377-4155-1 (pbk.)
    1. Freedom of the press. 2. Censorship. 3. Freedom of expression. 4. Mass media--Censorship. 5. Freedom of speech. I. Lerner, Alicia Cafferty. II. Lerner, Adrienne Wilmoth.
    Z657.F72 2009
    323.44'5--dc22
                                                            2009008221

Printed in the United States of America
1 2 3 4 5 6 7 13 12 11 10 09

Contents

Chapter 2: Artistic Expression and Censorship

Chapter 3: Internet Censorship

Chapter 4: Political Expression

Foreword

"The problems of all of humanity can only be solved by all of humanity."
—Swiss author Friedrich Dürrenmatt

Global interdependence has become an undeniable reality. Mass media and technology have increased worldwide access to information and created a society of global citizens. Understanding and navigating this global community is a challenge, requiring a high degree of information literacy and a new level of learning sophistication.

Building on the success of its flagship series, *Opposing Viewpoints*, Greenhaven Press has created the *Global Viewpoints* series to examine a broad range of current, often controversial topics of worldwide importance from a variety of international perspectives. Providing students and other readers with the information they need to explore global connections and think critically about worldwide implications, each *Global Viewpoints* volume offers a panoramic view of a topic of widespread significance.

Drugs, famine, immigration—a broad, international treatment is essential to do justice to social, environmental, health, and political issues such as these. Junior high, high school, and early college students, as well as general readers, can all use *Global Viewpoints* anthologies to discern the complexities relating to each issue. Readers will be able to examine unique national perspectives while, at the same time, appreciating the interconnectedness that global priorities bring to all nations and cultures.

Material in each volume is selected from a diverse range of sources, including journals, magazines, newspapers, nonfiction books, speeches, government documents, pamphlets, organization newsletters, and position papers. *Global Viewpoints* is truly global, with material drawn primarily from international sources available in English and secondarily from U.S. sources with extensive international coverage.

Features of each volume in the *Global Viewpoints* series include:

- An **annotated table of contents** that provides a brief summary of each essay in the volume, including the name of the country or area covered in the essay.

- An **introduction** specific to the volume topic.

- A **world map** to help readers locate the countries or areas covered in the essays.

- For each viewpoint, an **introduction** that contains notes about the author and source of the viewpoint explains why material from the specific country is being presented, summarizes the main points of the viewpoint, and offers three **guided reading questions** to aid in understanding and comprehension.

- **For further discussion** questions that promote critical thinking by asking the reader to compare and contrast aspects of the viewpoints or draw conclusions about perspectives and arguments.

- A worldwide list of **organizations to contact** for readers seeking additional information.

- A **periodical bibliography** for each chapter and a **bibliography of books** on the volume topic to aid in further research.

- A comprehensive **subject index** to offer access to people, places, events, and subjects cited in the text, with the countries covered in the viewpoints highlighted.

Global Viewpoints is designed for a broad spectrum of readers who want to learn more about current events, history, political science, government, international relations, economics, environmental science, world cultures, and sociology— students doing research for class assignments or debates, teachers and faculty seeking to supplement course materials, and others wanting to understand current issues better. By presenting how people in various countries perceive the root causes, current consequences, and proposed solutions to worldwide challenges, *Global Viewpoints* volumes offer readers opportunities to enhance their global awareness and their knowledge of cultures worldwide.

Introduction

> *"Everyone has the right to freedom of opinion and expression; this right includes freedom to hold opinions without interference and to seek, receive and impart information and ideas through any media and regardless of frontiers."*
>
> —*United Nations Declaration of Human Rights, Article 19, 1948*

Freedom of expression is the right to express one's opinions, feelings, and thoughts freely through writing, speech, art, protest, or other means without fear of reprisal. Freedom of expression encompasses several rights, including freedom of speech, freedom of the press, freedom of thought, freedom of information, and freedom of protest. It is the ability to stage a controversial art exhibit, to peacefully protest war by wearing black armbands to school without fear of suspension, to publish a newspaper article that criticizes the government, or to freely access information on the Internet. Freedom of expression is freedom from censorship.

Freedom of expression is an ancient concept, but for much of history free expression was rare. Around 450 BCE, Athenian playwright Euripides advocated free political speech, saying that true liberty was "when free-born men, having to advise the public, may speak free." Yet fifty years later, the philosopher Socrates faced trial and the death penalty for social and political speech in Athens.

Ancient Greece and Rome had vibrant political, academic, and art centers, but freedom of expression suffered in Europe during the Middle Ages. Dissent and free speech were most often tantamount to heresy or treason. The Catholic Church and strong kings largely controlled religion, art, and politics. Furthermore, there were fewer vehicles for free expression. The Magna Carta of 1215 said little about freedom of speech, but it did lay the foundation for freedoms of speech and political dissent in England.

In 1516, Dutch humanist philosopher Desiderius Erasmus, like Euripides, connected free expression to liberty, writing "in a free state, tongues too should be free." This connection between freedom of expression and liberty and democracy was strengthened during the eighteenth century Enlightenment, a time of renewed interest in science, mathematics, and classical philosophy. In 1770, Voltaire asserted that freedom of speech extended to all opinions—even those that one detests. Over the next two decades, the American and French revolutions would yield documents that first enshrined the modern concepts of freedom of expression. The 1789 French Declaration of the Rights of Man provided that the "free communication of ideas and opinions is one of the most precious of the rights of man. Every citizen may, accordingly, speak, write and print with freedom." In 1791, the First Amendment to the U.S. Constitution guaranteed the freedoms of speech, the press, assembly, religion, and the right to petition the government for the redress of grievances.

The concept of freedom of expression as a cornerstone for human rights expanded during the twentieth century, but so too did regimes that quashed freedom of expression. Communist and fascist regimes strongly restricted freedoms of speech, the press, and political dissent. After the defeat of Nazi Germany in World War II (1939–1945), the newly formed United Nations (UN) adopted resolution 59(I) stating that freedom of information was a "touchstone of all freedoms." In 1948, the UN issued the Universal Declaration of Human Rights. Article 18 of this document, which is still used as an international benchmark for human rights, provides for freedom of thought and conscience; Article 19 provides for freedom of expression.

The twentieth century also brought new ways to distribute information and new technologies for expression—radio, television, film, and the Internet. While freedom of expression is more commonly associated with freedoms of individual and group speech and freedom of the traditional press, the emergence of the Internet in the 1990s changed the way people share information. The Internet democratized information, making it freer, easier, and global. Many authoritarian governments that were able to closely control traditional media and outlets for expression have found the Internet more difficult to restrict.

China is one of many national governments that censors the Internet. Locked out by the Great Firewall of China, the colloquial name for Chinese Internet censorship, is information on democratic movements, political dissidents, Tibet, accusations of government corruption, and Western media reports on human rights abuses in the region. The international freedom of expression advocacy organization Reporters Without Borders asserts that China, Cuba, Iran, Maldives, Myanmar (Burma), North Korea, Syria, Tunisia, Uzbekistan and Vietnam all severely censor—or place an outright ban on—the Internet.

Though most western nations adopted laws guaranteeing a high degree of freedom of expression during the twentieth and early twenty-first centuries, there were several famous controversies that demonstrated the tensions between freedom of expression and censorship that cross cultural, religious, and national boundaries. In 1960, after a lengthy court battle in Britain, Penguin Books won the right to publish D.H. Lawrence's novel *Lady Chatterley's Lover*. The book remained banned by many schools and libraries, however. In 1989, author Salman Rushdie's book *The Satanic Verses* was banned by Islamic clerics, and death threats were made against Rushdie. In the 1990s, debate erupted over the U.S. National Endowment for the Arts sponsorship of explicit art works, including works from artists such as Robert Mapplethorpe. In 2004, militants murdered Dutch filmmaker Theo van Gogh after the release of his film about violence against women in Muslim societies. In 2005, publication of cartoons depicting the Muslim prophet Muhammad sparked protests and debate over censorship, cultural sensitivity, and political correctness.

Whatever the medium, freedom of expression is essential to democracy. It promotes government transparency, gives citizens access to information, and permits political dissent. However, even democratic governments place some restrictions on freedoms of expression. Many governments prohibit hate speech, speech that can incite violence, or speech that injures the reputation or safety of a person. Governments often restrict when and where a group may protest. Regulations may prohibit the airing of nudity or violence on television or film, or they may restrict advertisements by controversial products such as tobacco. Many governments restrict reporting on national security issues. These are all limits on pure freedom of expression. They are also examples of how people sometimes balance the need for freedom of expression with other concerns. This is a controversial and subjective process—what may be considered indecent by one person, nation, or culture may be acceptable to another. What is acceptable censorship to one may qualify as repressive to another.

While regulation of television content may be a debatable issue, there are some restrictions on freedom of speech that are widely recognized not only as censorship but also as violations of fundamental human rights. There are places where political dissent, explicit art, investigative journalism, or using the Internet can bring imprisonment or a death sentence. In parts of Asia, Africa, Latin America, the Middle East, and Russia, there are jailed journalists. Prisoners of conscience and political critics sit in prisons. Similarly, activists, outspoken citizens, journalists, cartoonists, photographers, lawyers, writers, and filmmakers have been persecuted, exiled, jailed, or killed. Freedom of expression may be a universal human right, but it is not yet universally protected.

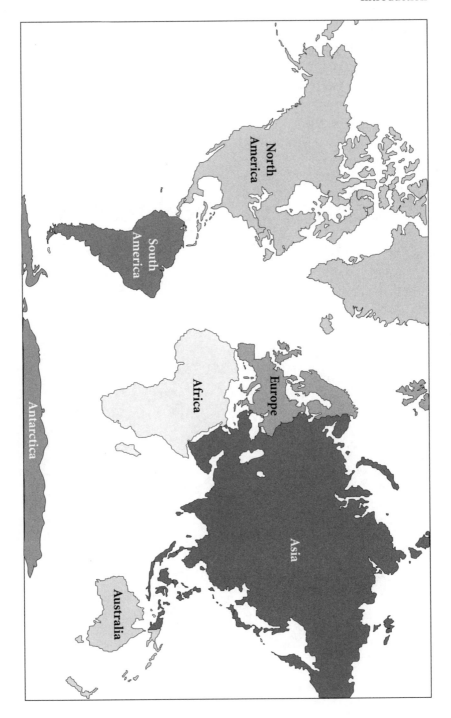

Freedom of the Press

Turkey Limits Writers' Freedom of Expression

Richard Lea

In the following viewpoint, Richard Lea reports on the interrogation and prosecution of best-selling Turkish novelist Elif Shafak. Shafak's novel, The Bastard of Istanbul, *was the first fictional work to be charged with the offense of "insulting Turkishness" under Article 301 of the Turkish criminal code. According to Lea, Shafak and her lawyer fought the charge on the grounds that dialogue of fictional characters cannot make an author liable for such a charge. If convicted, Shafak would have faced up to three years in prison; she was acquitted on September 21, 2006. Such author interrogations affected the eligibility of Turkey's accession into the European Union. However, as of April 2008, Article 301 has been amended and no longer includes the offense of "insulting Turkishness." Richard Lea has written for the British daily newspaper* The Guardian *for over a decade, specializing as a writer on Guardian Unlimited Books.*

As you read, consider the following questions:

1. According to Lea, approximately how many writers and journalists have been charged under Article 301?
2. According to Shafak, what are the two reasons she was charged under Article 301?

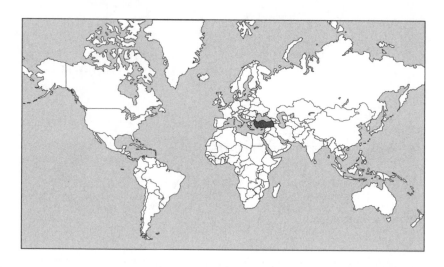

3. According to the article, what do Turkish nationalists think of Turkish writers who write in English?

"Nobody was expecting this," says bestselling Turkish novelist Elif Shafak. A decision in Istanbul's seventh high criminal court earlier this month reopened her prosecution on charges of "insulting Turkishness". She faces a maximum jail term of three years if convicted.

Shafak joins a roster of more than 60 writers and journalists to be charged under Article 301 of the Turkish criminal code since its introduction last year. University professors, journalists and novelists such as Perihan Magden, Orhan Pamuk and now Shafak have been charged under legislation drawn so broadly as to criminalise a wide range of critical opinions. Writers not only face the prospect of a three-year jail term, but the prosecutions also lay them open to a campaign of intimidation and harassment waged by rightwing agitators.

"The protests are maybe even more unnerving than the actual trial," Shafak told the *Guardian* today from her home in Istanbul. "Although their number is very limited they are very aggressive, very provocative." She describes crowds of protest-

Turkish Opinions on Freedom of Speech

The following 2007 survey question was directed to Turks regarding freedom of expression:

Suppose some day you were asked to draft a new constitution for a new country. As I read you a list of possible provisions that might be included in a new constitution, would you tell me whether you would probably agree or not agree with the inclusion of each of these provisions.

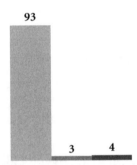

Freedom of speech—allowing all citizens to express their opinion on the political, social, and economic issues of the day.

- % Agree
- % Disagree
- % Don't know/Refused

TAKEN FROM: Magali Rheault, "Head Scarves and Secularism: Voices from Turkish Women," GALLUP.com, February 8, 2008. http://www.gallup.com.

ers slapping and jostling defendants both inside and outside the courtroom, shouting and throwing coins and pens.

The charges against Shafak open up new ground. She is not accused of "insulting Turkishness" because of her campaigning journalism or her academic work, but for remarks made by a fictional character in her latest novel, *The Bastard of Istanbul.*

The novel, which was originally written in English, was published in a Turkish translation in March 2006 and quickly became a bestseller. The novel follows four generations of women, moving between Turkey and the US to tell the story of an Armenian family and the descendants of a son left behind during the deportations, who converts to Islam and lives as a Turk. It is perhaps the first Turkish novel to deal directly with the massacres, atrocities and deportations that decimated the country's Armenian population in the last years of Ottoman rule.

Initial reactions to the book were mostly positive, and it went on to sell over 50,000 copies in less than four months. "I gave numerous readings, talks and book signings all over Turkey," explains Shafak. "Although the novel was difficult to digest for some people, in general the reception has been very positive."

But in June a nationalist lawyer called Kemal Kerincsiz filed a complaint in Istanbul's Beyoglu district court against Shafak, her publisher, Semi Sokmen, and her translator, Asli Bican. Shafak and her publisher argued during interrogation that the book was a work of literature and that comments made by fictional characters could not be used to press charges against an author.

"Most writers that are any good would get into trouble with the Turkish authorities."

"The interrogation went on for some time and eventually the prosecutor decided there was no element of insult and he dropped the case," says Shafak. But her relief was short-lived. Earlier this month the same lawyer took the case to a higher court, and ultimately managed to have the decision overturned. She is now confronted with a long and daunting legal process. A trial, with all the unwelcome attention from right-wing groups which that entails, is now inevitable.

It could not have come at a worse moment—she is six months pregnant. "From now on it is a long legal battle," she says. "The later stages of the pregnancy will probably coincide with the first stages of the trial."

Peter Ayrton, founder of Serpent's Tail, a publisher deeply committed to literature in translation, was unsurprised by the news of Shafak's prosecution. "Most writers that are any good would get into trouble with the Turkish authorities," he explains. "She's a very acerbic voice. Her novels are lively, episodic and innovative. She's obviously a feminist, and her work is obviously rooted in contemporary social conditions in Turkey."

According to Shafak, language has been at the heart of the process of creating a new nation state, with words of Persian, Arabic or Sufi origin being purged from the language in an attempt to break away from the Ottoman past.

Perhaps the time she spent abroad has given her a different perspective on Turkish life. She was born in Strasbourg, France in 1971 and spent her teenage years in Spain, before returning to Turkey to study social sciences. Four years ago she moved to the US, spending a year at the University of Michigan before her appointment as assistant professor at the University of Arizona. She now divides her time between the US and Turkey, where she has been touring the country to promote her new novel.

Shafak herself believes the charges were brought for two reasons: "The overt reason is my latest novel and the critical tone of the book. The latent reason is deeper and more complex. I have been active and outspoken on various 'taboo' issues, critical of ultranationalism and all sorts of rigid ideologies, including those coming from the Kemalist elite, and I have maintained a public presence on minority rights, especially on the Armenian question. It is a whole package."

Indeed, her fiction has always focused on social issues which Turks prefer to keep hidden, explains sociologist Muge Gocek, who translated the first of Shafak's novels to appear in the UK, *The Flea Palace*. "But she does so with humour, with grace, and without ever letting her characters lose their nobility of spirit," she adds.

The way Shafak deals with Turkey's past is also unique, continues Gocek, "both in terms of her knowledge of religious heterodoxy as well as her use of Ottoman words—these elements add layers of depth to her novels."

According to Shafak, language has been at the heart of the process of creating a new nation state, with words of Persian, Arabic or Sufi origin being purged from the language in an attempt to break away from the Ottoman past. "In the name of modernisation our language shrunk tremendously," she says.

"As a writer who happens to be a woman and attached to Islamic, as well as Jewish and Christian heterodox mysticism, I reject the rationalised, disenchanted, centralised, Turkified modern language put in front of me," she declares. "Today in Turkey, language is polarised and politicised. Depending on the ideological camp you are attached to, for example Kemalists versus Islamists, you can use either an 'old' or a 'new' set of words."

It is a choice she refuses to make, filling her writing with both "old" and "new" words. She says her fiction is like "walking on a pile of rubble left behind after a catastrophe. I walk slowly so that I can hear if there is still someone or something breathing underneath. I listen attentively to the sounds coming from below to see if anyone, any story or cultural legacy from the past, is still alive under the rubble. If and when I come across signs of life, I dig deep and pull it up, above the ground, shake its dust, and put it in my novels so that it can survive."

Catheryn Kilgarriff, co-director of her British publisher Marion Boyars, was also drawn to her use of old Turkish language, as well as her use of allegory and fable. "She's an extraordinary writer," she says, and an extremely exciting prospect for the future. "She's only 35 now and she's already mastered one or two different voices in her fiction. There's more to come."

It's a body of work which is building her a formidable reputation overseas. "She's doing astoundingly well," adds Kilgarriff, pointing out that Shafak's books have been taken up by the large chains and offered in three for two promotions—unusual treatment indeed for literature in translation.

Shafak has been published in Turkey, the US and Britain, though only two of her six novels are available in the UK at the moment. Since writing *The Flea Palace*, which was shortlisted for the Independent Foreign Fiction prize in 2005, she has begun writing in English—an act which has been seen by Turkish nationalists as a "cultural betrayal".

It was a choice motivated more by her passion for language, by the search for new modes of expression. "There are certain things I'd rather write in English, certain others I'd rather write in Turkish," she explains. "English, to me, is a more mathematical language, it is the language of precision. It embodies an amazing vocabulary and if you are looking for the 'precise word', it is right out there. Turkish, to me, is more sentimental, more emotional." English seems more suited for philosophy, analytical writing or humour, "but if I am writing on sorrow I'd rather use Turkish."

This is something that nationalists fail to understand, she says. "It is always us versus them, this or that. Nationalists cannot understand that one can be multilingual, multicultural, cosmopolitan . . . without feeling obliged to make a choice between them once and for all."

It is perhaps this instinct which lies at the heart of the wider conflicts taking place in contemporary Turkish society.

An increasingly urban Turkey has seen a broad cultural re-naissance over the last three decades, which has been consistently under-reported in the west. Voices in literature, academia and the arts have begun to examine subjects which have long been taboo, to raise questions about uncomfortable issues such as the role of women or the history of Turkey's Armenian minority.

But as this cultural resurgence has gained strength it has been met by a nationalist reaction.

"On the one hand there are the ones who want Turkey to join the EU, democratise further and become an open society," says Shafak, but on the other "are the ones who want to keep Turkey as an insular, xenophobic, nationalistic, enclosed society. And precisely because things are changing in the opposite direction, the panic and backlash produced by the latter group is becoming more visible and audible."

There are those who think that the prosecutions of leading writers under Article 301 are a sign that nothing is changing in Turkey, but Shafak thinks it is just the opposite: "Article 301 is being used more and more against critical minds precisely because things have been changing very rapidly in Turkey. The bigger and deeper the social transformation, the more visible the discomfort of those who want to preserve the status quo and the louder the backlash coming from them."

It's a reaction which has already cast doubt on to Turkey's accession into the EU. Earlier this month the European commissioner in charge of negotiations with Turkey urged the Turkish authorities to amend Article 301, reminding them that freedom of expression "constitutes the core of democracy" and is a "key principle" in determining a state's eligibility to join the EU.

It is too early to say what effect the trial will have on Shafak. She is determined that it will not influence her writing. "Next time I start a novel, I do not want to have qualms, fearing this or that topic might cause me yet another trouble," she says, adding that she is "much more daring" in her fiction than in her daily life: "While I am writing the urge to go on with the story outweighs any other concern that might cross my mind."

A date for her trial has not yet been fixed. For the moment all she can do is wait.

- *The Bastard of Istanbul* will be published in the US by Viking/Penguin in 2007.

- Elif Shafak's *The Gaze* was published in the UK earlier this month by Marion Boyars at £9.99.

Russian Journalists Risk Murder in the Face of Government-Censored Media

Matthias Schepp, Christian Neef, and Uwe Klussmann

In the following selection, Matthias Schepp, Christian Neef, and Uwe Klussmann report on the dangers of Russian journalism just weeks after the 2006 murder of native journalist Anna Politkovskaya. According to the authors, Politkovskaya's persistence in revealing government corruption made her one of approximately 260 Russian journalists to be murdered since the fall of the Soviet Union. The article recognizes that the journalists' murderers are often not found, and that the government is quick to dismiss the cases. Many of these instances are at most vaguely mentioned and then put to rest by Russian President Vladimir Putin, for fear of tarnishing Russia's global reputation. Schepp, Neef, and Klussmann are reporters for Spiegel, *a German international news magazine that publishes in print and on the Internet, in both German and English.*

As you read, consider the following questions:

1. According to Schepp, Neef, and Klussmann, under which Russian president was journalism "exciting, tough and impudent"?

Matthias Schepp, Christian Neef, and Uwe Klussmann, "Is Russia's Press Freedom Dead?" *Spiegel Online*, October 20, 2006. www.spiegel.de. © SPIEGEL ONLINE 2006. Reproduced by permission of the New York Times Syndicate.

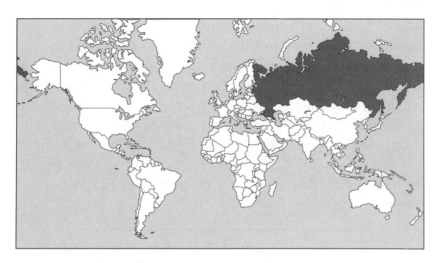

2. As recognized by the article, what did Russian President
   Vladimir Putin declare as his position when he took
   office in 2000?

3. According to the authors, former Russian President
   Mikhail Gorbachev condemned Politkovskaya's murder,
   asking for what action?

The gathering of Russians looks small in the hectic com-
motion of a busy street crossing in the heart of Moscow.
Fresh flowers have been placed by the building in front of
which journalist Anna Politkovskaya was gunned down on
Oct. 7 [2006], but the vigil doesn't look particularly impres-
sive. An old woman is there; so is an elderly professor with
thick horn-rimmed glasses. Twenty people have shown up,
which isn't a great showing in a city with a population of almost 11 million.

Politkovskaya had accused Russian President Vladimir Putin of "state terrorism" and called him a "KGB snoop," referring to his background as an agent for the Soviet intelligence
service. She accused the intelligence services now under his
command of committing abduction, torture and murder in
Chechnya. Such accusations aren't left unpunished in contem-

porary Russia. The politically powerful in the Kremlin accused Politkovskaya of besmirching her country's reputation.

She liked to wear old-fashioned wool sweaters. She was neither left- nor right-wing, but a kind of moral watchdog who kept an eye on Russian politicians. In some ways, she was to Russia what investigative journalist Seymour Hersh is to the United States: someone incorruptible and driven. Some of her colleagues thought she was fanatical and even biased. Politkovskaya tried to impose moral norms on post-Soviet Russia.

[Russian journalist Anna] Politkovskaya had accused Russian President Vladimir Putin of "state terrorism."

The 10-story tenement that Politkovskaya lived in, on Lesnaya Street 8, was built during the Stalinist era. It looks shabby. Its stone walls have been covered in a layer of yellow paint. They're plastered with posters, pieces of paper with poems written on them and a picture of Russian President Vladimir Putin. He's wearing sunglasses; his eyes are hidden.

"The State Has Taken Control of the Media"

On a picture of Politkovskaya displayed nearby, someone has written "Death of Freedom of the Press." The picture is framed in black. But the sign doesn't quite capture the truth, because Politkovskaya's journalistic activities had largely been curbed when she was still alive. She was banished from state-controlled public television and published only in the small newspaper *Novaya Gazeta*, which appears twice a week and has a readership of only about 100,000 people.

She was the daughter of a diplomat, but she wasn't diplomatic. Her investigative journalism lacked a proper audience and receptive context in Putin's Russia. And as a Russian journalist killed lately in unusual circumstances, she wasn't alone.

Just over a week after her murder, for example, the business chief of Russia's news agency, Itar-Tass, died of knife wounds in his own apartment in Moscow. Anatoly Voronin, 55, had worked for Itar-Tass for 23 years.

On a picture of Politkovskaya ... someone has written "Death of Freedom of the Press."

"The state has taken control of the media," Vladimir Ryzhkov, one of the last opposition politicians in the Russian Duma, explains. "And so no information gets through to the majority of Russians." This conclusion, drawn after 15 years of putative freedom of the press in Russia, could hardly be more bitter.

The Slow Stranglehold on Russian Media

During the first years after the fall of the Soviet Union, under President Boris Yeltsin, Russian journalism was exciting, tough and impudent. Then the oligarchs who had secured entire industrial sectors for themselves during the process of privatization bought up parts of the media landscape, from TV channels to the most important newspapers. They managed to supplement their new economic power with political power.

Putin came to office with the declared goal of restoring the Kremlin's political authority. Vladimir Gusinsky, the country's most important media entrepreneur, was arrested about five months later. His media holding company—including the TV channel NTW—was taken over by Gazprom, the state-controlled natural gas monopoly.

The Kremlin proceeded to let companies closely associated with the government purchase one publishing house after the other. In September, one such company acquired the Kommersant publishing group, distinguished by its high print runs and—until then—its critical stance towards the government.

The new owner Alisher Usmanov, formerly a leading functionary of the Communist Party's youth federation, is in charge of a Gazprom subsidiary. A billionaire and longtime acquaintance of Putin's spokesman Alexei Gromov, he promised "not to meddle with editorial policy." But then he immediately installed a Putin supporter as editor-in-chief and declared himself "entirely loyal to the state."

"Anyone who takes the place of Politkovskaya will take on a suicide mission."

Valery Yakov, the editor-in-chief of *Novye Izvestia*, reports that smaller non-conformist or critical papers are harassed by the authorities through surprising—and sometimes absurd—fire protection or health controls.

The result is that tough investigative journalism has become a rarity in Russia. "Anyone who takes the place of Politkovskaya will take on a suicide mission," says Yelena Tregubova, who has written a book describing her experiences as a Kremlin correspondent. A bomb exploded outside her front door shortly after the book was published.

261 Journalists Killed in Fifteen Years

According to Vsevolod Bogdanov, the chairman of the Russian Union of Journalists, 261 Russian journalists have been killed since the fall of the Soviet Union. Only 21 cases have been solved. And yet Putin had announced a "dictatorship of the law" when he took office in 2000. Today Russian journalists can relate to the part about dictatorship, but not to the one about the law.

Valery Ivanov, the editor-in-chief of the local paper in Togliatti, a center of the Russian auto industry and a city riddled with mafia [organized crime] clans, was shot in April of 2002. One-and-a-half years later, killers stabbed his successor Alexei Sidorov. Six journalists have died a violent death in Togliatti in eight years.

---

261 Russian journalists have been killed since the fall of the Soviet Union. Only 21 cases have been solved.

Yuri Shtshekotshichin, a writer and member of parliament, died in July of 2003. He may have been poisoned. Like Politkovskaya, he wrote for *Novaya Gazeta*. Paul Khlebnikov, editor-in-chief of the Russian edition of the business journal *Forbes*, was shot from a moving car in July 2004. Like Politkovskaya, he had researched the question of whether the funds provided by Moscow for reconstruction in Chechnya are being embezzled on a large scale. Three suspects had to be acquitted due to lack of evidence. Who ordered the assassination remains a mystery.

Murder is an everyday risk in other professions, too. The first vice director of the Russian central bank was killed by unknown assailants a month ago, and a branch manager of the foreign exchange bank was killed five days after Politkovskaya. Putin's presidential term ends in 2008, and his next-to-last year in power has seen Russia return to the general chaos of the 1990s, when hardly a week went by without an assassination.

"Coward Armed to the Teeth"

No one can say for sure who killed Politkovskaya, but Russian military officials who found themselves in court because of her articles would have an obvious motive. They include Igor Sechin, the vice director of the presidential administration and a man thought to wield considerable power behind the scenes in the Kremlin. Right-wing extremists are also known to have blacklisted Politkovskaya. Ramzan Kadyrov, the pre-

Journalist and Human Rights Activist Joan Smith Responds to the Murder of Anna Politkovskaya

Russia is the third-deadliest country in the world for journalists, according to the Committee to Protect Journalists, behind only Iraq and Algeria. This is happening now, on our doorstep, but a combination of circumstances—Putin's role in the so-called war against terror, and our dependence on Russian energy supplies—have inhibited western governments from the frank criticism his regime deserves.

Joan Smith,
"Putin's Russia Failed to Protect This Brave Woman,"
The Independent, *October 9, 2006.*

mier of Chechnya, is another suspect: Politkovskaya once called him a "coward armed to the teeth."

The Prosecutor General of Russia, Yuri Chaika, has declared the arrest of Politkovskaya's assassins one of his personal priorities. Yet Russia's public prosecutors are widely seen as anything but incorruptible. Nina Krushcheva, the granddaughter of former Soviet ruler Nikita Krushchev, even believes Chaika's declaration is "virtually a guarantee that the killers will never be found."

At least not the real ones. During his visit to the German city of Dresden last week, Putin set a tone for the investigations. Speaking at the Petersburg Dialogue, the annual Russian-German forum that was held in Dresden this year, Putin spoke of people who feel they are above Russian law and accused them of wanting to "sacrifice someone" in order to unleash a wave of "anti-Russian sentiment" in the world. It was his way of setting his sights on Russian oligarch Boris Berezovsky, the man who once helped him achieve political power and then fled into exile in London.

Putin's broad hint doesn't bode well for the upcoming parliamentary and presidential campaigns. The Kremlin might justify interference with the campaigns of the political opposition by arguing that they are being financed by people like Berezovsky—in order to ensure that the person who takes political power in Moscow in 2008 is someone Putin approves of.

Meanwhile, Berezovsky has issued a statement on Politkovskaya's murder from London implicitly accusing Putin of being responsible for her death. Berezovsky stated that while he doesn't think Putin had ordered her assassination, he nevertheless believes her death to be a "result of his policies."

According to Putin's logic, the idea behind the spectacular murder wasn't to eliminate a meddlesome journalist, but to damage his own reputation. Does that mean the political system in which so many journalists are murdered shouldn't be an object of scrutiny?

Tension in Dresden

The former leader of the Soviet Union, Mikhail Gorbachev, has been known for his cool relationship with former KGB director Putin. Gorbachev was in Dresden at the same time as Putin; he acted as co-chairman of the Petersburg Dialogue. He condemned the murder of Politkovskaya and called for an independent "journalistic investigation."

But Gorbachev, master of the vague statement, also qualified his condemnation. Plenty of things go on in other countries, he suggested darkly, adding that not all the research undertaken by Politkovskaya's paper was "well founded." (The former Communist ruler, however, has owned shares of *Novaya Gazeta* since June.) Besides, Gorbachev went on to say, Russia is "firmly on the road to democracy."

Putin was visibly upset in Dresden that the death of a journalist in Russia could interfere with his country's image. He seemed tense and irritable. "It's all very bad for us," one Russian diplomat murmured, adding, however, that it was time for Russia to stop taking lessons from the West in matters of freedom of the press.

And so Putin emphasized that Politkovskaya's "influence on political life" in Russia was "very minor," repeating this assertion no less than three times. "This murder inflicts far more damage on Russia," he said, "on the current authorities in Russia and in Chechnya . . . than her publications did."

The statement was intended as a jab at the West. But what Putin said—on the day of Politkovskaya's burial, no less—was both impious and cynical.

German representatives at the Petersburg Dialogue work group which focused on media issues were also struck by the attitude of their Russian colleagues. They all seemed more offended than shocked or disturbed. Politkovskaya had just been honored with a minute of silence when a well-known St. Petersburg senator demanded that the same be done for the most recent journalist casualties in Afghanistan. The message was clear: The Politkovskaya case has no symbolic value—it's just one of many comparable cases in the world.

Russia's Future

The German press took a different view, even as Russian visitors to Dresden wanted to return to their pre-established agenda. The critical comments in the press were interpreted by the Russian representatives as a "concerted attack from the other side of the barricade." Russia's ambassador in Berlin, Vladimir Kotenev, spoke of "German campaign journalism." A TV reporter from Russia's "First Channel"—which is known to be sympathetic to Putin's government—even drew a historical comparison between contemporary German newspapers and the media propaganda of the Soviet Union during the 1970s. He concluded that the only reason Russians have a good relationship to Germany is that they don't read the German press.

A liberal Moscow-based editor-in-chief later commented that the squabbling in Dresden prompted by Politkovskaya's death amounted to "a conversation among deaf mutes." But more than that, it seems to have been a lesson on the differences between two journalistic cultures—a lesson that left a fresh feeling of helplessness over how to deal with Russia.

Not only has Anna Politkovskaya been murdered . . . but many hopes for Russia's future have been quashed as well.

The roughly 3,000 people who turned out for Politkovskaya's burial in Moscow last week seemed helpless, too. Not a single well-known politician from Putin's leadership was there. The only prominent politicians who showed up had been in power under Putin's predecessor, Boris Yeltsin.

Russian writer Viktor Yerofeyev was reminded of his time as a political dissident in the Soviet Union. Not only has Anna Politkovskaya been murdered, he said, but many hopes for Russia's future have been quashed as well.

Kenyan Press Freedom Was Compromised in the Wake of the 2007 Election

Susan Linnee

After announcements about the outcome of Kenya's 2007 presidential election, riots broke out in many parts of that country, fueled by ethnic tensions between supporters of the incumbent and those of the opposition leader. In the following viewpoint, Susan Linnee reports on the complicated relationship between the media and the Kenyan government. In the aftermath of the election, the internal security minister for newly reelected president Mwai Kibaki banned television and radio field broadcasts as well as mass demonstrations. But the situation goes beyond government censorship, Linnee reports. Many Kenyan journalists had developed close relationships with the politicians, even working on their campaigns. These affiliations called into question the neutrality of many media sources, Linnee reports. In addition, Linnee points out that the ethnic conflicts in Kenya pose dangers for journalists—members of the media have faced threats both from official sources and from members of certain ethnic communities. Linnee has been a West Africa correspondent for the Associated Press for twenty-five years. Global Journalist online magazine identifies issues of global press freedom and serves journalists around the world.

Susan Linnee, "Restrained," Globaljournalist.org, April 30, 2008. 2008 Global Journalist. Reproduced by permission.

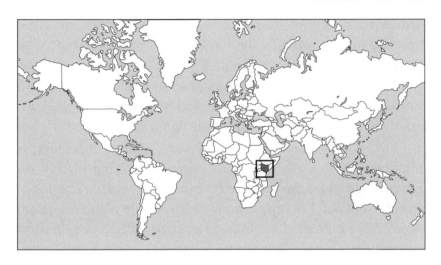

As you read, consider the following questions:

1. According to Linnee, what message did internal security minister John Michuki give to reporters after attacking Kenya's media outlet the Standard Group several years before the 2007 riots?

2. According to the article, instead of identifying the names of certain ethnic groups, Kenyan media outlets would use what types of euphemisms?

3. As identified by the article, what was the name of the media workshop held a month after the riots?

For years, the Kenyan media observed the conflicts in Sudan, Somalia, Ethiopia, Uganda, Rwanda, Burundi and Congo as though their regional neighbors were somehow in another—and very dangerous—world far from their peaceful nation.

Kenya received refugees from countries with other conflicts. Trucks bearing the seal of the International Committee of the Red Cross traversed the East African nation carrying tents, relief food and other supplies to the victims of war and genocide, and specialized agencies of the United Nations brought millions of dollars into the country and employed hundreds of Kenyans in their regional offices that dealt with the faraway disasters.

Kenyan diplomats and negotiators mediated a settlement to the 20-year civil war in Sudan and helped pull together yet another transitional government in Somalia.

But, the Kenyan media rarely sent its own reporters or photographers to cover regional violence, relying instead on international agencies for their news of the world. The monstrous events of 1994 in Rwanda, a 50-minute plane ride from Nairobi, were as alien to Kenyans as they were to people most everywhere.

2007 marked 44 years of independence for Kenya.

Post-Election Pandemonium

Then, on the evening of December 29, [2007] as members of the Electoral Commission of Kenya [ECK] droned out results of the December 27 presidential election, the most hotly contested in the country's 44 years of independence, dozens of people ran riot through the main street of the normally quiet western town of Kisumu, the stronghold of the main opposition candidate Raila Odinga, a member of the Luo tribe. Within hours, the businesses on the street had been set afire and looted as guests watched from the upper floors of the Kisumu Hotel. Then the rioters began to go after those who might have dared to vote for President Mwai Kibaki—or who were simply members of his Kikuyu ethnic group, the largest of the 42 in Kenya.

Early results broadcast nationwide over radio and television had indicated that Odinga was in the lead. Then, as results came in from Kibaki's home turf in Central Province, it began to look as though the tide had turned. Pandemonium broke out in the Kenyatta International Conference Center in downtown Nairobi where the votes were being tallied and read out. ECK chairman Samuel Kivuitu then halted counting until the following day.

In the mid-afternoon of Sunday December 30, Kivuitu first appeared on, then disappeared from the live TV broadcasts, then suddenly appeared again on the state-run channel KBC to declare Kibaki the winner; a few hours later, he was sworn in on another live KBC broadcast in what appeared to be a hastily convened ceremony. A short time later when other live broadcasts showed riots breaking out in the sprawling slums that surround much of Nairobi and where many Odinga supporters live, the internal security minister declared a ban on all TV and radio broadcast from the field and banned all mass demonstrations as well. The minister, John Michuki, a longtime ally and business friend of Kibaki, was the same man who several years earlier had led an unexplained attack on The Standard Group, the nation's oldest media outlet that includes the Standard newspapers and KTN television. His words then to reporters were: "when you find a snake, you cut off its head."

Kenyan Media Sources

In the past decade, the Kenyan media world has undergone tremendous expansion, particularly in television and radio. Although not entirely devoid of the urge to exercise ultimate control over the airwaves, Kibaki's economically laissez-faire government that took power in 2003 licensed several terrestrial TV stations, including the brand new 24-hour K-24, to bring the country's total to seven, as well as dozens of FM radio stations, many of them in local languages.

The newspaper world of the *East African Standard* and the *Daily* and *Sunday Nation* also grew with the addition of two "down market" dailies—*Nairobi Star* and *Daily Metro*—and a business newspaper, the *Business Daily*. The latter two are the

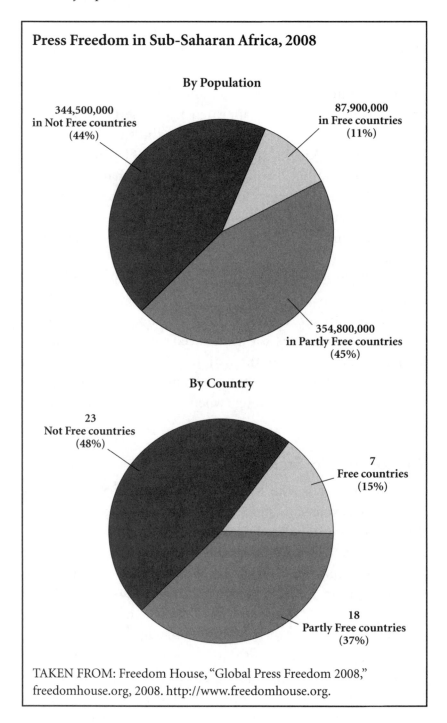

Press Freedom in Sub-Saharan Africa, 2008

By Population

344,500,000
in Not Free countries
(44%)

87,900,000
in Free countries
(11%)

354,800,000
in Partly Free countries
(45%)

By Country

23
Not Free countries
(48%)

7
Free countries
(15%)

18
Partly Free countries
(37%)

TAKEN FROM: Freedom House, "Global Press Freedom 2008,"
freedomhouse.org, 2008. http://www.freedomhouse.org.

most recent additions to the stable of the Nation Media Group, whose principal shareholder is the Aga Khan Fund for Economic Development.

"[Journalists] had become too close to the politicians."

The Relationship Between Politics and the Media

Mugumo Munene has been a journalist for seven years and recently became news editor at the *Sunday Nation* after returning from a five-month fellowship at the *Kansas City Star*.

Referring to the violent reaction that followed the declaration of Kibaki's victory, Munene said it should have been possible to foresee at least some aspects of the events that followed from the way the campaigns were conducted and how journalists got involved.

"There is a very high likelihood that [Kenyan journalists] haven't covered certain stories because of what has been going on, and how it would affect reporters [in the local news bureaus across the country]."

"All this started way back last year as politicians were preparing their campaigns. It became apparent when they invited journalists to become their media consultants; they worked at newspapers during the day and moonlighted at night for the politicians," he said. "We noticed this in their stories. They had become too close to the politicians."

"The editors' job got harder because we had to look out for hidden biases, rather than just editing the copy. No one was prepared for what happened after the results of the election were announced. Reporters still kept their biases, and there is more pressure on editors to keep taking out the biases."

Munene said the newspaper's management sent e-mails warning staff against bias and inciting ethnic tensions. But no one was fired, he said, "because bias is difficult to prove."

In addition to its headquarters in Nairobi—the nerve center and main focus of all the Kenyan media—the Nation Media Group has five bureaus throughout the country and between 50 and 100 staff and stringers. It is well known in Kisumu, Nakuru, Eldoret, Mombasa and Nyeri who works for which newspaper, radio and TV station. The Standard Group and KTN have similar bureaus.

"There is a very high likelihood that we haven't covered certain stories because of what has been going on, and how it would affect reporters there," Munene said.

During the election campaign and the post-election crisis in which at least 1,000 people were killed and another 300,000 displaced, the major newspapers and the TV stations have not identified the various ethnic groups by name in an attempt to avoid inciting violence. Euphemisms like "a certain community" or "people from a certain part of the country" or "those who voted for a certain candidate" abound.

Although the conflict has been widely described both in the Kenyan and international media as tribal, the origins are far more complex and have much more to do with the perceived—and real—inequality in the distribution of wealth and power in post-colonial Kenya. And readers and listeners know which group is doing what to which, other group anyway.

During the election campaign and the post-election crisis . . . at least 1,000 people were killed and another 300,000 displaced. . . .

The Ban Is Lifted but Censorship Is Not

The day after the ban on live broadcasting was lifted on February 5, Samuel Poghisio, the new information minister, said the government was tracking information passed through the print and electronic media as well as via the Internet and text messages "to rein in" content that could endanger peace by exacerbating ethnic tensions or spreading hate. He said the focus would be on "errant media houses" as well as international correspondents and foreign news agencies. But, Poghisio said it is not at all clear whether the government has the means to carry out such surveillance.

Towards the end of January, the photo of a young child sitting near the body of its mother, who had been hacked to death in the Rift Valley, was circulated by e-mail through Kenyan media outlets but never showed up in print—in Kenya. It was on the front page of the January 29 government-owned New Vision newspaper in neighboring Uganda.

[Many Kenyan journalists] told of receiving threats related to how they or their papers, radios or TV stations were perceived to be covering the events.

Ida Jooste, the resident journalism adviser in Kenya for Internews, the U.S.-based international organization that works to provide "information access for everyone," says young Kenyan radio announcers, many of whom were hired for the new local language FM stations based solely on the quality of their voices, "were shocked at what they had unwittingly done or were not aware of doing" in broadcasting ethnic stereotypes and spreading what were little more than rumors. Few if any have any background in journalism.

Kenyan Media Is Concerned for Its Future

A month after the violence broke out, Internews held a workshop—30 Days in Words and Pictures: Media Response in Kenya during the Election Crisis—to take stock of the situation. Jooste said 78 of the 80 people invited turned up, and many of them told of receiving threats related to how they or their papers, radios or TV stations were perceived to be covering the events.

Salim Amin, a Kenyan of South Asian background who is involved in setting up a 24-hour all-Africa TV channel, has been covering news throughout the region for more than a decade. He said initially he and his TV crew "found the police and the protestors to be quite accommodating, but as things got heated up, then we found that we were being target by police and their tear gas . . . but not the demonstrators."

"But then I was asked if A-24 were up and running, how would it work with local crews? It's a good question," he said. "Now you can only send certain tribes to certain areas. In this particular story I've been proved very wrong; for the first time in Kenya, being a local journalist has been a disadvantage rather than an advantage . . . this has severely compromised coverage by the local media here."

China's Media Restrictions Are Substantial but May Decrease as the Economy Expands

Carin Zissis and Preeti Bhattacharji

In the following viewpoint, Carin Zissis and Preeti Bhattacharji explain the issue of media freedom in China. The authors cover such aspects as what the official media policy in China is, what the major Chinese censoring agencies are, and how China controls foreign media influence. The authors describe the conflict between the public's growing desire for more information and the government's control of content in order to maintain power. They assert that, while government suppression of the media is still substantial and widespread, media freedom has expanded slightly and will continue to do so. Zissis, a journalist, photographer, and communications specialist is a Web site staff writer for the Council on Foreign Relations. Bhattacharji is a specialist on Asia for the Council on Foreign Relations. The Council on Foreign Relations is an American nonpartisan foreign policy membership organization that publishes articles, reports, and books on the subject of foreign policy and overall international issues.

As you read, consider the following questions:

1. According to Zissis and Bhattacharji, where did Reporters Without Borders rank China in 2007 in its press freedom index?

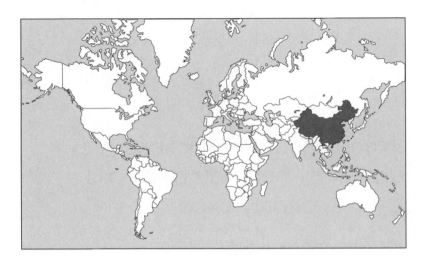

2. As identified by the authors, how many journalists were sent to jail in China in 2007, giving it the reputation as the "world's biggest jailor of reporters"?

3. According to Northeast Asia media expert Ashley W. Esarey, what is the primary arena for freedom of speech in China?

The 2008 Summer Olympics in Beijing have drawn international attention to censorship in China. Watchdog groups say the preexisting monitoring system piles on new restrictions, and the government continues to detain and harass journalists. But the country's burgeoning economy allows greater diversity in China's media coverage, and experts say the growing Chinese demand for information is testing a regime that is trying to use media controls in its bid to maintain power.

The Official Media Policy in China

As China becomes a major player in the global economy, authorities in Beijing are trying to balance the need for more information with their goal of controlling content as a means to maintain power. CFR [Council on Foreign Relations] Senior

Fellow Elizabeth C. Economy says the Chinese government is in a state of "schizophrenia" about media policy as it "goes back and forth, testing the line, knowing they need press freedom—and the information it provides—but worried about opening the door to the type of freedoms that could lead to the regime's downfall." Although President Hu Jintao was expected to be more liberal than his predecessors, his administration has pursued a media policy that involves increased regulations as well as the arrest and prosecution of journalists. Bob Dietz, Asia Program Coordinator for the Committee to Protect Journalists (CPJ), says this "hard swing to the conservative side" will likely be the direction taken as long as Hu is in power.

But in spite of a crackdown under Hu, China's media is undergoing a process of commercialization, leading to growing competition, diversified content, and an increase in investigative reporting by Chinese news agencies. According to a government report, there are more than two thousand newspapers, over eight thousand magazines, and some three hundred and seventy-four television stations in the country. China also has over 150 million Internet users and, despite restrictions governing online content, both domestic and international stories that censors would prefer to control slip through government information firewalls. Only state agencies can own media in China, but there is creeping privatization as outlets subcontract administrative operations to the private sector. Northeast Asia media expert Ashley W. Esarey says it is also likely the Internet will play a role in Chinese media reform, because its "absolute control has proven difficult, if not impossible."

How Free Is Chinese Media?

The watchdog group Reporters Without Borders ranked China 163 out of 168 countries in its 2007 index of press freedom. China's constitution affords its citizens freedom of speech and press, but the document contains broad language that says Chinese citizens must defend "the security, honor, and interests of the motherland." Chinese law includes media regulations with vague language that authorities use to claim stories endanger the country by sharing state secrets. Journalists face harassment and prison terms for violating these rules and revealing classified matter. The government's monitoring structure promotes an atmosphere of self-censorship; if published materials are deemed dangerous to state security after they appear in the media, the information can then be considered classified and journalists can be prosecuted.

The Primary Censoring Agencies in China

Several government bodies are involved in reviewing and enforcing laws related to information flowing within, into, and from China, but the two primary censoring agencies are the General Administration of Press and Publication (GAPP) and the State Administration of Radio, Film, and Television (SARFT). GAPP licenses publishers, screens written publications (including those on the Internet), and has the power to ban materials and shut down outlets. SARFT has similar authority over radio, television, film, and Internet broadcasts.

But the most powerful monitoring body is the Communist Party's Central Propaganda Department (CPD), which coordinates with GAPP and SARFT to make sure content promotes and remains consistent with party doctrine. Xinhua, the state news agency, is considered by press freedom organizations to be a propaganda tool. The CPD gives media outlets directives restricting coverage of politically sensitive topics—such as protests, environmental disasters, Tibet, and Taiwan—which could be considered dangerous to state security and party control. The CPD guidelines are given to heads of media outlets, who in turn kill controversial stories and decide how delicate topics will be covered. Journalists who do not follow the rules face reprisals in the workplace. Publicizing the CPD guidelines invites punishment, too, as in the case of Shi Tao, a journalist detained in 2004 and serving a ten-year sentence for posting an online summary describing the CPD's instructions for how to report about the fifteen-year anniversary of events at Tiananmen Square [when the Chinese army shot and killed hundreds of peaceful protesters].

China's primary censoring agencies are the General Administration of Press and Publication (GAPP) and the State Administration of Radio, Film, and Television (SARFT).

How Does China Exert Media Controls?

The Chinese government uses different means of intimidation to control the media and induce journalists to censor themselves rather than risk punishment. Censorship tactics include:

Dismissals and demotions. One of the most common punishments, say watchdog groups, is to fire or demote editors and journalists who publish articles objectionable to the CPD.

Libel. Government officials occasionally use accusations of libel as a way to intimidate media outlets and publishing houses. Cases range from a journalist charged with libel for writing pieces critical of Communist Party leaders on foreign Web sites to an author whose book about the extortion of farmers by local officials was banned after one of the officials sued him and his publishing house.

One of the most common punishments . . . is to fire or demote editors and journalists who publish articles objectionable to the CPD [the Communist Party's Central Propaganda Department].

Fines. In August 2007, China passed the "Emergency Response Law," which bans the spread of unverified information

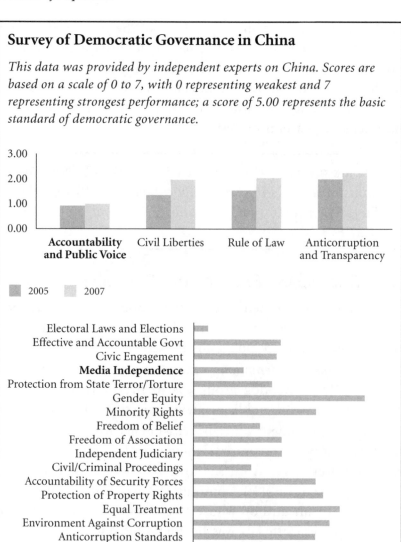

Survey of Democratic Governance in China

This data was provided by independent experts on China. Scores are based on a scale of 0 to 7, with 0 representing weakest and 7 representing strongest performance; a score of 5.00 represents the basic standard of democratic governance.

TAKEN FROM: Freedom House, "Countries at the Crossroads 2007 : Selected Comparative Data from Freedom House's Annual Survey of Democratic Governance," freedomhouse.org, 2007. http://www .freedomhouse.org.

regarding riots, disasters, and other emergencies. Originally, the law threatened to fine media sources up to $12,500 for violations, but it was redrafted with more ambiguous language before it was passed.

Closing news outlets. News organizations that cover issues the CPD considers classified face closure. In a 2005 report, the *People's Daily* said three hundred and thirty-eight publications were shut down the previous year for printing "internal" information.

Imprisonment. China imprisoned twenty-nine journalists in 2007, making it the world's biggest jailor of reporters for the ninth year running, according to CPJ. Almost two-thirds of the jailed reporters were arrested for materials published on the Internet. One incarcerated foreign correspondent, Ching Cheong of Singapore's *Straits Times,* was arrested in 2005 while reporting about leaders within the Chinese Communist Party. Cheong was sentenced to five years in prison, plus one year's deprivation of political rights. His arrest had a chilling effect on press freedom in Hong Kong, where he was based.

"China knows it cannot afford to tamper with the flow of economic data, and that is where it will receive the most external pressure."

Controlling the Influence of Foreign Media

China requires foreign correspondents to get permission before making reporting trips within the country and reporters often face harassment if they cover delicate issues.

As part of its bid to host the 2008 Olympics, China promised to relax constraints and "be open in every aspect to the rest of the country and the whole world." In January 2007, Chinese Premier Wen Jiabao signed a decree that allows foreign journalists to report without permits before and during the Beijing Games. The decree also allows foreign journalists to interview any individual or organization as long as the interviewee consents. The new guidelines came into effect on January 1, 2007, and will last through October 27, 2008.

But critics accuse China of reneging on its Olympic promise. The Foreign Correspondents Club of China reports that one hundred and eighty foreign correspondents were detained, harassed, or attacked in China in 2007 despite the nominally relaxed regulations. In addition, China continues to filter foreign (and domestic) content on the Internet—in many cases using technology provided by U.S. companies such as Yahoo!, Microsoft, and Google.

One of the largest foreign uproars came when Beijing introduced regulations in September 2006 requiring foreign wire services to distribute news through Xinhua instead of selling economic information directly to clients. CFR's Economy says the restrictions had less to do with media control than with a bid by Xinhua to cut into wire services' profits. The move was "brazen," says Dietz, because even as Beijing continues prosecuting journalists who cover controversial social issues, "China knows it cannot afford to tamper with the flow of economic data, and that is where it will receive the most external pressure." But despite the pressure that foreign groups place on China, experts say that criticism coming from outside China will have little effect on policy.

Journalists Find Ways Around Media Control Measures

Despite the systematic control of news in China—the U.S. State Department estimates China has between thirty thousand and fifty thousand Internet monitors—editors and journalists find ways to get news past the censors. Esarey says the primary space for freedom of speech in China is the blogosphere, where journalists use humor and political satire to criticize the Chinese government. In mainstream media, editors find ways to test the rules as readers in China's flourishing economy demand hard news, says Dietz, and journalists covering social issues their editors won't publish will post stories online, where the news will be released into cyberspace even if the original post is removed.

Dietz predicts press freedom "will expand to meet the needs and demands not just of the government but of the society." Chinese media broke the news about official suppression of information about the 2003 SARS outbreak in Beijing. Similarly, after toxic chemicals leaked in to a river and contaminated drinking water in the northeast city of Harbin in 2005, newspapers and Web sites criticized government response, demanded greater transparency, and posted photos of area residents stockpiling bottled water.

In Slovakia and Throughout Eastern Europe, Media Freedom Has Declined

The Economist

In the following viewpoint, The Economist *magazine addresses decreasing media freedom in Slovakia and several other ex-Communist countries in Eastern Europe. A new Slovakian law effective June 2008 requires newspapers to print replies from people named in articles who feel their reputation or privacy has been impinged. This law states that unless the editor of the newspaper involved can convince a court to rule in favor of not publishing a response, he or she must do so to avoid substantial fines for breaking this law. As observed by* The Economist, *the Slovakian government believes that the law will "make the media more responsible" for the content it publishes. While the authors acknowledge issues regarding the impartiality of the Slovakian media, they express concern that the law could be abused by the government. The authors also identify other Eastern European countries that have recently faced dwindling press freedom. Based in London,* The Economist *is an English-language weekly newsmagazine with an emphasis on global affairs.*

"Less Free Speech: Tough Laws and Interfering Politicians Are Shrinking Media Freedom," *The Economist*, April 24, 2008. www.economist.com. Republished with permission of The Economist Newspaper Group, conveyed through Copyright Clearance Center, Inc.

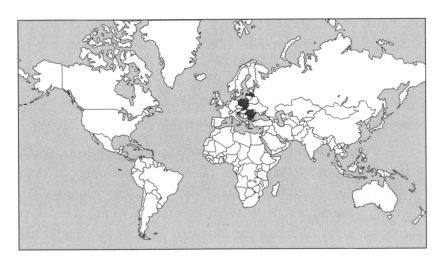

As you read, consider the following questions:

1. As identified by the authors, what was risked by Slovakia's lack of media freedom with its authoritarian government in the 1990s?

2. What is the statement America's ambassador to Bucharest, Nicholas Taubman, made concerning Romania's defamation law?

3. According to the article, how is public broadcasting sometimes used by Eastern European politicians?

Pick up a Slovak newspaper, and you will find it a quick, if depressing, read. The main dailies have in recent weeks been appearing with blank, black-framed front pages, in protest at a new media law that will give anyone mentioned in an article sweeping rights to an equally prominent rebuttal. International media watchdogs have sharply attacked the law. They are worried by declining media freedom across Eastern Europe.

2008 Slovakian Media Law Challenges the Authority of Press Editors

Slovakia's new law comes into force on June 1st [2008]. If somebody referred to in a newspaper story complains, the onus will be on the editor to print their response unless he can persuade a court to rule otherwise. A rebuttal may not be accompanied by additional editorial comment. A refusal to print one can lead to big fines. Right-of-reply rules are common in several European countries, but Slovakia's law is the most punitive and, potentially, arbitrary.

The government, a populist-nationalist coalition, insists that the law will make the media more responsible. "It does not jeopardise freedom of the press. It merely upgrades the interest of the public above the interest of the publishers," says Marek Madaric, the culture minister. The Slovak media are not above reproach. A forthcoming report by the Open Society Institute, a group financed by George Soros, talks of "plagiarism, refusal to make corrections and hidden conflicts of interest."

[Slovakia's new media law] does not jeopardise freedom of the press. It merely upgrades the interest of the public above the interest of the publishers.

Yet there is reason to worry about how Slovakia's prime minister, Robert Fico, may use the law. He has a prickly relationship with the media, which have harried his government for inertia and alleged corruption. He declines to give interviews and sometimes even to take questions from critical journalists, and he has called some daily newspapers "prostitutes". Some journalists recall the dark days of the 1990s, when the authoritarian government of Vladimir Meciar (who is now Mr Fico's junior coalition partner) jeopardised the country's accession to the European Union and NATO [North Atlantic Treaty Organization]. (To be fair, Mr Fico's predecessor, Mikulas Dzurinda, who was lionised abroad for his reforms, clashed with the press, and was once accused of bugging media opponents.)

"Slovakia's Front Page Protests"

All Slovakia's major daily newspapers were published with blank front pages on Thursday, March 27 [2008], in protest of the government's controversial attempt to revise the Press Code. Their covers each featured just a short, identical notice to readers listing their most serious objections to the proposed Press Code, which has attracted criticism from both Slovak publishers and the international community.

The papers—*Sme, Pravda, Hospodárske Noviny, Novy as, Plus Jeden De* and *Új Szó*, which are all members of the Periodical Press Publishers' Association—printed the same text under the headline "Seven Sins of the Press Code".

"Do you want someone other than the editors to prepare your favourite newspaper for you?" asked the dailies in their protest statement. "The new Press Code from the workroom of the governing coalition is heading in this direction."

Beata Balogová and Ľuba Lesná,
"Seven Sins of the Press Code," The Slovak Spectator,
March 31, 2008. www.spectator.sk.

Ex-Communist Countries Experience Regression of Media Freedom

Slovakia's new law is the most conspicuous in the region. But arbitrary legal constraints on press freedom are worrisome elsewhere, too. In Bulgaria defamation of public figures (a broad category that can include prominent businessmen) is a crime that can be punished with a fine. Journalists can also be sued for infringing somebody's "honour and dignity". As many as 60 cases went to court in 2006, and a further 100 in 2007.

In Romania the constitutional court last year [2007] restored a tough defamation law that criminalises "insult", though the effect on press freedom pales beside the ownership of most of the mainstream media by three politically active tycoons, plus political interference in public broadcasting. America's ambassador to Bucharest, Nicholas Taubman, has suggested that "legislators should strengthen their own accountability . . . rather than try to hamper the efforts of a free media to exercise its legitimate role in Romania, either through criminalizing journalistic efforts or otherwise intimidating independent media."

All this is bad news in a region that used to take pride in its reborn freedom. And bad laws are only part of the picture. In the annual report of Freedom House, a New York-based lobby group, to be published on April 29th, the ex-Communist countries show the biggest relative decline in media freedom in the world, chiefly because of a perceived politicisation of public broadcasting. The drop is larger than in Asia, Africa and Latin America.

Ex-Communist countries show the biggest relative decline in media freedom in the world.

Thus Latvia's score slips from 19 to 22, after the government appeared to lean on public television to cover Russia more politely. Slovakia's falls from 20 to 22, Slovenia's from 21 to 23, and Poland's from 22 to 24. Mr Soros's media-watchers echo Freedom House's judgment. "Politicians think these public broadcasters should be 'theirs'," says Marius Dragomir, who is publishing a clutch of detailed reports on public-service broadcasting in the region. With EU [European Union] accession safely negotiated, politicians now feel able to exploit the fruits of power more freely. Politicised public broadcasting is a useful tool to manipulate the voters, especially when commercial television is run by friendly tycoons.

Such trends are troubling. But everything is relative. Recently a Russian newspaper, *Moskovsky Korrespondent*, published a widespread rumour about the supposed relationship of President Vladimir Putin with a comely gymnast, Alina Kabaeva. After Mr Putin lambasted the tabloid, which is a sister publication to *Novaya Gazeta*, an opposition paper, it was promptly shut down by its publisher. Such an event would be unimaginable in the new EU members from central and eastern Europe. For now, at least.

Italian Journalists Self-Censor to Avoid Recriminations from Government Leaders

Kirstin Hausen

In the following viewpoint, Kirstin Hausen addresses attitudes toward media freedom in Italy. According to Hausen, though outspoken journalists are rare in Italy, when they do step forward to criticize the Italian government, they are often threatened with a lawsuit. Such threats are not issued very often however, politicians' prevasive power over the media usually leads to journalistic self-censorship. Hausen points out that the Italian public is mostly apathetic regarding the lack of investigative journalism. Hausen is based in Milan, Italy, as a reporter for Deutsche Welle, Germany's international media broadcaster using the Internet, television, and radio.

As you read, consider the following questions:

1. According to Hausen, outspoken Italian journalist Marco Travaglio's comments on television about Senate President Renato Schifani led to what reaction by Schifani?

2. How does Travaglio explain the self-censorship of Italian journalists?

3. As identified by Hausen, who appoints the top positions at Italian state television channel RAI?

Kirstin Hausen, "Italian Journalists Muzzle Their Criticisms," dw-world.de, May 25, 2005. Reproduced by permission.

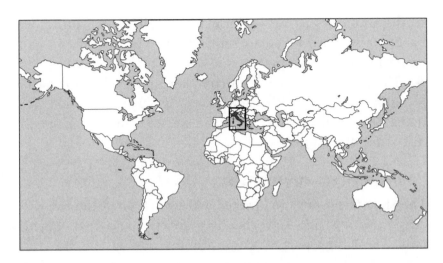

Television host Fabio Fazio knew what he was getting into when he invited journalist Marco Travaglio to be a guest on his show. Travaglio doesn't mince words, especially when it comes to criticizing Italian politicians. Over the years, Travaglio has gained the reputation of being Italy's most outspoken journalist.

On Fazio's show, he spoke openly about a topic that everyone more or less knew about, but which hadn't been openly discussed: the past mafia [organized crime] connections of current Senate President Renato Schifani.

The fact that Travaglio dared to speak openly about the subject caused a furor in Italy, with Schifani threatening to sue for slander, a common weapon used against outspoken journalists in Italy.

Many Journalists Steer Clear of Criticism

Even during the live television interview, host Fabio Fazio distanced himself from the accusations. He looked into the camera, an embarrassed expression on his face, and apologized to newly re-elected premier and media magnate Silvio Berlusconi. Berlusconi is not a fan of airing such uncomfortable truths about his party supporters, yet politicians from other parties also have taken to ranting daily in talk shows and newspapers on the topic.

The real scandal has been completely pushed to the background: namely that the newly elected Senate president had mafia ties. Yet it was Travaglio who was denounced for openly discussing the matter.

Politicians vs. Journalists

The state television broadcaster RAI, which aired the live discussion with Marco Travaglio, has publicly apologized to Schifani. The ruling parties welcomed the apology as did Giovanna Meladri, the communication director for the opposition. No one from opposition leader Walter Vetroni's party defended Travaglio. But this doesn't bother Travaglio. He stands by his reporting.

"I am a journalist and I don't care what politicians say about me," Travaglio said. "Journalists have to tell people the truth and that is what I have done."

Travaglio understands his journalistic responsibilities and he has a work ethic that many Italian journalists seem to have lost long ago. Travaglio said he sees it as a tragedy that Italian newspapers only write about what the television news reported on the day before. Politicians then pick up on these reports and react if they don't like what they see or hear.

Many Italians are simply not interested in knowing about the underhanded dealings of the political class.

Politicians stand ready to "muzzle journalists," Travaglio said. Journalists know it and "restrain themselves accordingly."

The Italian Public Is Largely Apathetic

For certain topics, censorship isn't even necessary as journalists practice self-censorship to avoid trouble. Plus, there's no

A Questionnaire About Press Freedom

These questions were taken from a questionnaire for compiling a 2007 world press freedom index. The answers to such questions helped to determine Italy's ranking as 35th in the world.

Over the period, was/were there (yes/no):

- An official prior censorship body systematically checking all media content?

- Media outlets censored, seized or ransacked? (how many?)

- Routine self-censorship in the privately-owned media? Give this a score from 0 (no self-censorship) to 5 (strong self-censorship)?

- Subjects that were taboo (the armed forces, government corruption, religion, the royal family, the opposition, demands of separatists, human rights, etc)?

- News that was suppressed or delayed because of political or business pressure?

- Do the media report the negative side of government policies?

- Do the media report the negative side of actions of powerful companies or their owners?

- Do the media undertake investigative journalism?

Reporters Without Borders,
"Questionnaire for Compiling a 2007 World Press Freedom Index,"
www.rsf.org.

clamor for the type of investigative reporting done by Travaglio. Many Italians are simply not interested in knowing about the underhanded dealings of the political class. Writer Nanni Ballestrini calls it a "weak dictatorship."

Italians are complicit in the set-up, Ballestrini said.

In fact, there's grudging admiration of a clever politician, such as Berlusconi, who can hold on to power even while under investigation.

But that doesn't mean Berlusconi wants his legal maneuverings spoken about in the media. At his own television channels, a call is all it takes to spike critical news reports.

At the state television station RAI the influence is less direct, but nevertheless noticeable. In Italy the ruling parties decide the top positions at the television station, which means they can put their cronies in charge. The new government will decide on how to fill these posts very soon.

England's Press Must Seek a Balance Between Free Speech and Respect for Others

Simon Jenkins

In the following viewpoint, English journalist Simon Jenkins asserts that printing cartoons of the Muslim prophet Muhammad, in Denmark and elsewhere in Europe, was insensitive and wrong. Jenkins argues that rather than asserting the newspapers' free speech rights, the printing of such cartoons insults a religion and culture that forbids depicting Muhammad because the Qur'an condemns idolatry. Jenkins believes that in order to protect free speech, media outlets must demonstrate the ability to edit with restraint and sensitivity. He declares that in England, the government has proven all too willing to censor the press if that institution fails to regulate itself. Jenkins is a former editor and writer for The Times *and a former political editor of* The Economist. *He presently writes for* The Sunday Times *and* The Guardian. *Jenkins was knighted for his services to journalism in 2004.*

As you read, consider the following questions:

1. Jenkins claims that newspapers have a responsibility to determine a balance of what elements?

2. What does Jenkins claim is the consequence if the press does not "practice self-discipline"?

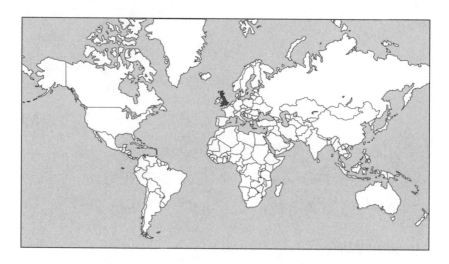

3. According to Jenkins, what is "the best defense of free speech"?

I think, therefore I am, said the philosopher. Fine. But I think, therefore I speak? No way.

Nobody has an absolute right to freedom. Civilisation is the story of humans sacrificing freedom so as to live together in harmony. We do not need Hobbes to tell us that absolute freedom is for newborn savages. All else is compromise.

The Printing of Muhammad Cartoons Was Inflammatory

Should a right-wing Danish newspaper have carried the derisive images of Muhammad? No. Should other newspapers have repeated them and the BBC teasingly "flashed" them to prove its free-speech virility? No. Should governments apologise for them or ban them from repeating the offence? No, but that is not the issue.

A newspaper is not a monastery, its mind blind to the world and deaf to reaction. Every inch of published print reflects the views of its writers and the judgment of its editors. Every day newspapers decide on the balance of boldness, offence, taste, discretion and recklessness. They must decide who is to be allowed a voice and who not. They are curbed by libel laws, common decency and their own sense of what is acceptable to readers. Speech is free only on a mountain top; all else is editing.

Despite Britons' robust attitude to religion, no newspaper would let a cartoonist depict Jesus Christ dropping cluster bombs, or lampoon the Holocaust. Pictures of bodies are not carried if they are likely to be seen by family members. Privacy and dignity are respected, even if such restraint is usually unknown to readers. Over every page hovers a censor, even if he is graced with the title of editor.

To imply that some great issue of censorship is raised by the Danish cartoons is nonsense. They were offensive and inflammatory. The best policy would have been to apologise and shut up. For Danish journalists to demand "Europe-wide solidarity" in the cause of free speech and to deride those who are offended as "fundamentalists . . . who have a problem with the entire western world" comes close to racial provocation. We do not go about punching people in the face to test their commitment to non-violence. To be a European should not involve initiation by religious insult.

A newspaper is not a monastery, its mind blind to the world and deaf to reaction.

The Importance of Respecting Religion, Race, and Culture in the Press

Many people seem surprised that a multicultural crunch should have come over religion rather than race. Most incoming migrants from the Muslim world are in search of work and security. They have accepted racial discrimination and cultural subordination as the price of admission. Most Europeans, however surreptitiously, regard that subordination as reasonable.

What Muslims did not expect was that admission also required them to tolerate the ridicule of their faith and guilt by association with its wildest and most violent followers in the Middle East. Islam is an ancient and dignified religion. Like Christianity its teaching can be variously interpreted and used for bloodthirsty ends, but in itself Islam has purity and simplicity. Part of that purity lies in its abstraction and part of that abstraction is an aversion to icons.

Of all the casualties of globalism, religious sensibility is the most hurtful.

The Danes must have known that a depiction of Allah as human or the prophet Muhammad as a terrorist would outrage Muslims. It is plain dumb to claim such blasphemy as just a joke concordant with the western way of life. Better claim it as intentionally savage, since that was how it was bound to seem. To adapt Shakespeare, what to a Christian "is but a choleric word", to a Muslim is flat blasphemy.

Of all the casualties of globalism, religious sensibility is the most hurtful. I once noticed in Baghdad airport an otherwise respectable Iraqi woman go completely hysterical when an American guard set his sniffer dog, an "unclean" animal, on her copy of the Koran. The soldier swore at her: "Oh for Christ's sake, shut up!" She was baffled that he cited Christ in defence of what he had done.

Likewise, to an American or British soldier, forcibly entering the women's quarters of an Arab house at night is normal peacekeeping. To an Arab it is abhorrent, way beyond any pale. Nor do Muslims understand the West's excusing such actions, as does [British Prime Minister] Tony Blair, by comparing them favourably with those of [former Iraqi President] Saddam Hussein, as if Saddam were the benchmark of international behaviour.

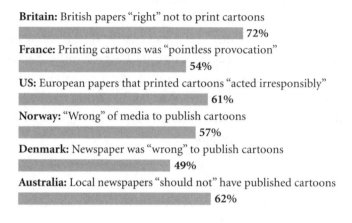

Poll Shows Disapproval of Publishing Muhammad Cartoons in Western Countries

Britain: British papers "right" not to print cartoons
72%

France: Printing cartoons was "pointless provocation"
54%

US: European papers that printed cartoons "acted irresponsibly"
61%

Norway: "Wrong" of media to publish cartoons
57%

Denmark: Newspaper was "wrong" to publish cartoons
49%

Australia: Local newspapers "should not" have published cartoons
62%

TAKEN FROM: Angela Stephens, "Publics in Western Countries Disapprove of Muhammad Cartoons," worldpublicopinion.org, February 16, 2006. http://www.worldpublicopinion.org.

It is clearly hard for westerners to comprehend the dismay these gestures cause Muslims. The question is not whether Muslims should or should not "grow up" or respect freedom of speech. It is whether we truly want to share a world in peace with those who have values and religious beliefs different from our own. The demand by foreign journalists that British newspapers compound their offence shows that moral arrogance is as alive in the editing rooms of northern Europe as in the streets of Falluja. That causing religious offence should be regarded a sign of western machismo is obscene.

Government Involvement in Press Issues

The traditional balance between free speech and respect for the feelings of others is evidently becoming harder to sustain. The resulting turbulence can only feed the propaganda of the right to attack or expel immigrants and those of alien culture.

And it can only feed the appetite of government to restrain free speech where it really matters, as in criticising itself.

There is little doubt that had the Home Office's original version of its religious hatred bill been enacted, publishing the cartoons would in Britain have been illegal. There was no need to prove intent to cause religious hatred, only "recklessness". Even as amended by parliament the bill might allow a prosecution to portray the cartoons as insulting and abusive and to dismiss the allowed defence that the intention was to attack ideas rather than people.

The traditional balance between free speech and respect for the feelings of others is evidently becoming harder to sustain.

The same zest for broad-sweep censorship was shown in Charles Clarke's last anti-terrorism bill. Its bid (again curbed by parliament) was to outlaw the "negligent", even if unintended, glorification of terrorism. It wanted to outlaw those whose utterances might have celebrated or glorified a violent change of government, whether or not they meant to do so. Clarke proposed to list "under order" those historical figures he regarded as terrorists and those he decided were "freedom fighters". The latter, he intimated, might include Irish ones. This was historical censorship of truly Stalinist ambition. By such men are we now ruled.

That a modern home secretary should seek such powers illustrates the danger to which a collapse of media self-restraint might lead. Last week there were demands from some (not all) Muslim leaders for governments to "apologise" for the cartoons and somehow forbid their dissemination. It was a demand that Jack Straw, the foreign secretary, commendably rejected. It assumed that governments had in some sense allowed the cartoons and were thus in a position to atone for them. Many governments might be happy to fall into this trap and seek to control deeds for which they may have to apologise. The glib assumption of blame where none exists, feeds ministerial folie de grandeur, as with Blair's ludicrous 1997 apology for the Irish potato famine.

Self-Regulation and Discipline Protect a Free Press

In all matters of self-regulation the danger is clear. If important institutions, in this case the press, will not practise self-discipline then governments will practise it for them. Ascribing evil consequences to religious faith is a sure way of causing offence. Banning such offence is an equally sure way for a politician to curry favour with a minority and thus advance the authoritarian tendency. The present Home Office needs no such encouragement.

Offending an opponent has long been a feature of polemics, just as challenging the boundaries of taste has been a feature of art. It is rightly surrounded by legal and ethical palisades. These include the laws of libel and slander and concepts such as fair comment, right of reply and not stirring racial hatred. None of them is absolute. All rely on the exercise of judgment by those in positions of power. All rely on that bulwark of democracy, tolerance of the feelings of others. This was encapsulated by Lord Clark in his defining quality of civilisation: courtesy.

Too many politicians would rather not trust the self-restraint of others and would take the power of restraint onto themselves. Recent British legislation shows that a censor is waiting round every corner. This past week must have sent his hopes soaring because of the idiot antics of a few continental journalists.

The best defence of free speech can only be to curb its excess and respect its courtesy.

Thai Media Are Censored by the Government

Marwaan Macan-Markar

In the following viewpoint Marwaan Macan-Markar describes Thailand's media censorship, which is dictated by the country's junta, or military-appointed government. According to Macan-Markar, the junta specifically did not want television or radio stations to broadcast statements by Thailand's ousted prime minister Thaksin Shinawatra or members of his party. Web sites have also come under severe restrictions. Macan-Markar reports that the Thai media community and human rights groups are concerned for the future of Thai broadcasting as well as for the country's democracy. Macan-Markar is a reporter based in Bangkok, Thailand, for Inter Press Service News Agency, an organization that produces articles and analyses about such topics as global journalism and worldwide communications.

As you read, consider the following questions:

1. According to human rights groups, what promise did Thailand's junta make when it took over the country?

2. According to Macan-Markar, what action occurred in three Thai provinces after the junta obtained power?

3. While Thaksin Shinawatra was prime minister, what tactics did he use to censor the media?

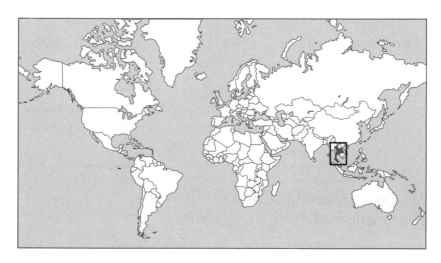

At a leading television station, the censor's scissors stand ready to snip out any reference to Thailand's ousted prime minister Thaksin Shinawatra or members of his Thai Rak Thai (Thais Love Thai) party.

"You cannot quote a press statement by Mr. Thaksin word for word or even what his party releases," Clare Patchimanon, a news anchor on a morning current affairs programme for Channel Three TV, tells IPS [Inter Press Service News Agency]. "There is an editorial policy to be careful about what goes on the air."

Since last week [January 2007] she and other radio and other TV broadcasters have come under pressure from the country's junta [military dictatorship] to restrict local media exposure to Thaksin, who was ousted in the Sep. 19 [2006] military coup.

The bluntness of the junta's order conveyed its new, tough stance in dealing with the former, twice-elected leader, who has been forced to live in exile. "I want to ask every television channel and every radio station not to broadcast messages or statements of the former prime minister and leaders of the past ruling party," General Winai Phattiyakul, a ranking member of the junta, told media representatives on Jan 10 [2007].

"If they don't listen," he added, "you can kick them out of your station or if you can't use your judgement, I will use mine to help you run your station."

Sections of the local print media that welcomed the country's 18th coup as a chance to restore Thai democracy . . . are not so sure now.

Media Censorship Conflicts with the Restoration of Thai Democracy

As the junta has dropped its mask of appearing benign, it is also losing friends. Sections of the local print media that welcomed the country's 18th coup as a chance to restore Thai democracy that Thaksin had undermined are not so sure now.

"We are not very happy with this meddling. The Thai press has expressed its displeasure," says Kiatichai Pongpanich, senior editor of *Khaosod*, a Thai-language daily. "This is not a very normal situation."

Human rights groups are also firing broadsides at the junta, pointing that its menacing approach to the local broadcasters goes against the pledges it had made to justify the putsch, among which was a promise to help restore Thai democracy from the abuse it had suffered during Thaksin's five-year government.

"We are concerned by this disturbing trend to control the broadcast media," Sunai Phasuk, Thai researcher for the global rights lobby Human Rights Watch, told IPS. "This is counterproductive to the promise they made to introduce a democratic culture."

The uproar over the limits placed on the broadcast medium—the news outlets with the largest reach in this country of 64 million people—has overshadowed the increasing restrictions that have been placed on the new media, such as Web sites.

Statement by the Group "19 September Network Against Coup D'etat"

We want to state that:

1. We do not accept the political power of the military to intervene in the democratic system. . . .

2. We ask the military to return to their divisions and bases, and stop their involvement in the coup d'etat process. . . .

3. We would like people who oppose the coup d'etat to express their thoughts through:

   • using the colour black as the symbol of opposition (wear black shirts, ties or armbands)

   • turning on the headlights of their cars during the day

   • organising talks and discussions on democracy within their family, company or organisation, among friends or at their school or university.

Asian Human Rights Commission, "Thailand: Resistance to Junta Growing Inside Thailand; Media Blackout 'Impossible,' AHRC says," AHRCHK.net, September 22, 2006.

During the first four months since the coup, the number of Internet Web sites that have been blocked in Thailand have jumped by "over 500 percent," notes a statement by a newly established media watchdog, Freedom Against Censorship in Thailand (FACT). "No identification of Web sites blocked has ever been disclosed to the public nor do (the) government agencies disclose which criteria they use to block."

By mid-January, according to FACT, the number of Web sites blocked by the Ministry of Information and Communication had reached 13,435, a dramatic rise from the 2,475 sites that had been blocked in mid-October.

"Inevitably, the coup group is having to show more and more of its real face, which like any other dictatorship is ugly," Basil Fernando, head of a regional rights group, Asian Human Rights Commission, said this week. "The figures on Internet censorship speak for themselves."

The Junta Tightens Its Grip on Thai Media

But the Council for National Security (CNS), as the junta calls itself, had already fired warning shots about how much media freedom it would tolerate within days of the coup, when it went after community radio stations in Thailand's north and north-eastern provinces, where Thaksin had a huge following. In the provinces of Chiang Mai, Chiang Rai and Mae Hong Son, some 300 community broadcasters were forced into silence a day after the junta grabbed power.

Television stations in Bangkok, like the one where Clare, the anchor, works, had to put up with other pressures, such as armed soldiers in each station. Channel Three, for instance, had a regular presence of armed soldiers in the main control room for the first month following the coup, after which the soldiers remained on the watch, but without weapons.

Censorship, whatever the motives behind it, is against all democratic principles.

It was a form of intimidation aimed at preventing Thaksin or his supporters taking to the airwaves to mount a media campaign and challenge the authority of the junta. Such heavy-handed measures contrasted with the more subtle tactics—such as using money and threatening to stop advertisements—that Thaksin employed while in government to silence the media.

The junta's expanding campaign against the Thai media is being viewed by analysts here as one more self-inflicted wound as it appears to be losing its way in a political environment that is growing increasingly fragile. Four months after it took power, the junta has succeeded in creating more dissension and divisiveness—an atmosphere it had pledged to end through a coup that was aimed at unifying this Southeast Asian country.

"Since the coup, government censorship has only focused on breaking communication channels between Thaksin and the Thai people," Philippe Latour, Southeast Asia representative for Reporters Without Borders, the global media watchdog, told IPS. "Censorship, whatever the motives behind it, is against all democratic principles and it is shocking when it comes from a government that promised to bring back democracy within 12 months."

Periodical Bibliography

The following articles have been selected to supplement the diverse views presented in this chapter.

The Economist "Less Free Speech; The Press in Eastern Europe," April 26, 2008.

Gady A. Epstein "Dark Journalism. (Journalistic Ethics in China)," *Forbes*, vol. 182, no. 1, July 21, 2008.

Adam Liptak "The First Amendment: A User's Guide. The Most Famous Words in the Constitution Protect a Host of Rights for Americans—and Still Spur Debate After 215 Years," *New York Times Upfront*, October 9, 2006.

Owen Matthews and Anna Nemtsova "War with the Media; Moscow's Crackdown on Independent News Outlets Harkens Back to the Dark Days of the Soviet Era," *Newsweek International*, July 2, 2007.

Greg Mitchell "NYT Explores New Restraints on Images from Iraq," *Editor & Publisher*, July 25, 2008.

Philippines News Agency "Right to Reply Not Meant to Curtail Press Freedom," October 9, 2008.

Richard Stengel "No One Gets a Blank Check," *Time*, July 10, 2006.

U.S. News & World Report "5 Countries with the Freest Press; The United States Ranks 36th out of 173 Countries, Says Advocacy Group Reporters Without Borders," October 27, 2008.

Fred Weir "Murder in Moscow: The Death of a Courageous Woman," *New Internationalist*, November 2006.

CHAPTER 2

Artistic Expression and Censorship

Malaysian Artists Begin to Take Their Work from Home to Public Galleries

Sonia Kolesnikov-Jessop

In the following viewpoint, Sonia Kolesnikov-Jessop describes the political transition Malaysia began in 2004 of allowing the display of avant-garde art in public places. Kolesnikov-Jessop explains that prior to 2004, notably under former prime minister Mahathir Mohamad, art that conveyed dissent was not given space in galleries alongside more conservative art. Instead, according to Kolesnikov-Jessop, such art was shown from artists' homes and empty office buildings. According to a major Malaysian artist, Wong Hoy Cheong, his art was censored not in the conventional sense, but by being blocked from a public space because of its subject matter. Kolesnikov-Jessop has lived in Singapore since 2001, and reports on such topics as culture, business, and lifestyle.

As you read, consider the following questions:

1. According to Kolesnikov-Jessop, what is the subject matter of Wong's artworks that made their first public appearance in Malaysia in 2004?

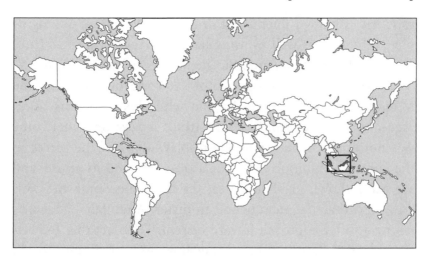

2. According to visual artist Nadiah Bamadhaj, before 2004, how did many Malaysian contemporary visual artists manage to publicly show their work involving political statements?

3. What does Wong assert is a Malaysian law that compromises the country's freedom of expression?

Among the works on display at the National Art Gallery in Kuala Lumpur is a picture alphabet collaged from the texts of Hitler's *Mein Kampf* and *The Malay Dilemma*, a book criticizing Malay culture by former prime minister Mahathir Mohamad. There are also tiles made of pulped Asian history books for visitors to step on, and a "Tapestry of Justice," consisting of more than 10,000 thumbprints of those who called for the repeal of Malaysia's Internal Security Act, which allows the police to put any individual deemed a threat into preventive detention. They are part of "Wong Hoy Cheong," a powerful retrospective of the contemporary artist's work.

Art Comes Out of Hiding for Public Display

Wong, the most high-profile Malaysian artist on the international scene, has exhibited widely in Asia, Australia and Europe. He is known for mixing drawing, installation, photography and video, as well as using natural materials such as fruit, plants and even cow dung. But he has never been prominently displayed in Malaysia—until now. A vocal opponent of the Mahathir regime, Wong says that while his work was never "censored" as such, there were "strong suggestions" that some was not appropriate for public display. Many of the pieces in the current exhibition are critical of power and its abuse, and are being shown in Malaysia for the first time. Some view this as a sign that the new prime minister, Abdullah Badawi, is taking a softer approach toward dissent. "The fact that the National Art Gallery is hosting the show adds credibility to the view that the Mahathir era is gone," says Valentine Willie, a gallery owner who is also Wong's art dealer.

Many of the pieces in the [2004] exhibition are critical of power and its abuse, and are being shown in Malaysia for the first time.

Under Mahathir's domineering rule, Malaysian artists weren't exactly prohibited from exploring themes like human rights or authoritarian rule; they just weren't offered any place to exhibit such works. Often they were forced to show in private spaces like empty office blocks. Nadiah Bamadhaj, a visual artist who has had work rejected by public galleries, has looked into subjects like the 1960s confrontation between Malaysia and Indonesia and the creeping influence of money politics in the ruling Malaysian political party. She says that many contemporary visual artists "got away" with their political statements by abstracting them or encoding them in "visual forms that are less accessible to some people." Still, she says, "the transition between Mahathir and Abdullah is an important one for local artists, as it reshuffled who heads ministries and [art] institutions, and this could have an important

---

A Response to Malaysia's Strict Film Censorship as Stifling to Artistic Expression

... [C]ensorship negates creativity. Freedom of expression is a necessary tool for a creative artist. If you stifle that, you kill the talented local industry. . . .

... [M]ovies are a work of art and have to be seen in the light of total impact. Ideally, on a big screen. And this is possible if the board just cuts pornography and violence and leaves the rest to us. . . .

Vasanthi Ramachandran, "Unkind Malaysian Cuts?"
New Straits Times *(Malaysia), February 6, 2005.*

---

impact on what gets shown in public spaces." Perhaps not co-incidentally, the head of the National Art Gallery, who was perceived as fairly conservative, recently retired.

Government Transition Shows a Greater Acceptance of Artistic Expression

Besides Wong's, other socially challenging works have also been recently displayed in Malaysia, like Fariza Azlina Isahak's pastel-colored installation of Muslim women posed seductively while doing household chores. One of Wong's works never before exhibited in Malaysia is "Vitrine of Contemporary Events," an installation of objects found in demonstrations. It includes judges' wigs and police batons made of cow dung, videos showing women singing a patriotic song and a copy of the Malaysian Constitution printed on paper made from vacuum-cleaner refuse. The piece was created in 1999 after the arrest of former deputy prime minister Anwar Ibrahim. "There seems to be a broader acceptance that oppositional views can coexist," says Wong.

Still, he says, it's too soon to determine whether Malaysia has actually become freer under Abdullah. "Some people do want to craft that image, but more time is needed to see whether it's just spin-doctor talk or there are changes in actual fact," says Wong. "Let's see whether the fight against corruption continues. The government has said that the ISA [Internal Security Act] will never be removed, so things haven't really changed; they just appear to have changed." But as his show helps make clear, seeing is believing.

Iranian Law Prohibits Women from Singing Solo in Public

Freemuse

In the following viewpoint, Freemuse reports on the views of world-renowned Iranian setarist and conductor Mohammad-Reza Lotfi. Lotfi has publicly criticized the Iranian law that segregates musical performances of men and women. According to the author, in Iran women are forbidden to publicly perform solo vocal acts unless for an all-female audience. The author explores the cultural reasons behind gender segregation in Iran. Freemuse is an independent international organization that promotes freedom of musical expression through musicians and composers.

As you read, consider the following questions:

1. According to this Freemuse article, what type of musical performance are women allowed to participate in if men are present in the audience?
2. According to Nakissa Sedaghat, what effect does the religious law of Iran have on the segregation of women?
3. How did Yvonne Buchheim capture the self-censorship of an Iranian female vocalist during her film project?

"I don't believe in the segregation of men and women because I think that art is not just for only one gender. However, if Iran's constitutional law and political system have

"Setar Master Openly Critisized Ban on Female Vocalists," Freemuse.org, April 28, 2008. Reproduced by permission.

prohibited women from solo vocal performances in public, despite my desire, I have to respect the law as an Iranian citizen."

The renowned Iranian traditional musician and conductor Mohammad-Reza Lotfi stated this when he held a press conference on 19 April 2008 to promote a concert series of his at Tehran's National Grand Hall in May, wrote the *Tehran Times*.

He was also quoted as saying, "it is unfair to use women as carriage wheels of men."

"I don't believe in the segregation of men and women because I think that art is not just for only one gender."

The 61-year-old setar virtuoso is often referred to as the "father of new aesthetics in Persian music" and a "living musical legend", and because of his recognition a statement like this is highly controversial in a country where solo performances by female singers are currently permitted only in concerts restricted to all-female audiences, and where women singers are allowed to appear only in choral performances if the audience includes males.

Iranian Women Are Involved in the Underground Rap Music Scene

Rap is forbidden in Iran. . . .

Despite the prohibition on women singing in public, female rappers . . . dot the Iranian music landscape. . . .

In late April [2007], when the authorities launched a crackdown on fashion, they also took steps to curb underground music. Some musicians were jailed, their recording studios raided and shut down. Most singers were freed once they promised not to produce any more underground music.

Anuj Chopra, "Iranian Rap Music Bedevils the Authorities,"
U.S. News and World Report, *March 12, 2008. www.usnews.com.*

Mohammad-Reza Lotfi returned home to Iran from the United States after 20 years in 2006, and soon after he reopened the Mirza Abdollah Music School and the Ava-ye Sheida Institute recording company. Then he founded the Women's Sheida—a band with women musicians and a male singer, and the Sheida of Restoration—a band which performs and records Lotfi's rearrangements of Iranian traditional pieces.

"Protection" Against Sexuality of Women

"In Iran, the revolution has resulted in a bizarre model of Islamic democracy. The government is elected and thus is supposed to represent the will of the people. However, since all laws have to ultimately be approved by a council of Islamic clerics who sit at the top of the pyramid of power, it is very difficult to make any legal reforms no matter who you vote for in the elections. All bills deemed to be non-Islamic are rejected and the Islamic clerics' interpretation of the Koran cannot be challenged."

This explanation can be found in an article entitled 'Divine Discrimination' by Nakissa Sedaghat on Iranian.com. The author of the article argues that the religious law in Iran imposes unequal treatment of women. Segregation of women, she writes, is a result of the religious law:

"Gender segregation is a result of religious leaders' cultural viewing of women as sexual beings whose sole goal in life is to tempt men so that they can fulfill their own sexual desires. This cultural view affects the interpretation of Islamic and Jewish edicts on 'modesty' of women, resulting in the wearing of the veil in Iran and of long skirts and wigs or hats for Ultra-Orthodox women in Israel. This imposed 'uniform' results in a further segregation of women when they venture out of their homes into the public sphere. It succeeds in dehumanizing them, and robbing them of their individuality. . . .

"Women are encouraged culturally and religiously, if not by law, (yet), to remain in the confines of their homes to fulfill their 'duties', as wife and mother. Also, for the same reasons of 'protection' against sexuality of women, women are not allowed to sing in public in Iran."

The religious law in Iran imposes unequal treatment of women.

A Case of Self-Censorship

Yvonne Buchheim from University of the West of England visited Iran while she was working on a project where she invited people from different ages and social backgrounds to perform a song of their choice in front of her video camera. The project, entitled 'The Song Archive Project', examined contemporary song culture in a visual art context, based on a suggestion that the cultural identity of a people is reflected through their song tradition. In Iran she came across a woman singer in a mountain village, and one evening the woman's family invited her to join their party. Yvonne Buchheim wrote:

"Family gatherings are a fundamental structure to the social relations in Iran and family bonds are very close. The young woman was a music student and performed a beautiful song in the garden as her family looked on. As the evening progressed everybody started dancing (officially men and women should be dancing in separate rooms) and even some alcohol appeared (strictly forbidden). The woman grew more and more quiet and finally asked me to erase her singing. I was shocked at the self-censorship but I followed her request to black out her singing. However I kept all the video footage before and after the song recording, the chatter and applause, and on reflection I realized that the absence commented far more deeply on the social dynamic of this culture."

Vietnam Attempts to Censor Artists

Roger Mitton

In the following viewpoint, Roger Mitton reports on Vietnam's attempt to control artistic expression among its people while broadening interactions with other countries. Mitton relates that soon after the ruling Communist Party's cultural commission visited local art exhibits in Hanoi, the subject matter was condemned and the displays closed. Mitton explains that as Vietnam becomes more integrated into the global community, citizens are exposed to a greater variety of cultural expression, and Vietnam's censors are kept busy. The government has adopted a two-pronged strategy to rein in artistic expression, Mitton points out, punishing those who displease the Communist Party and rewarding those who adhere to party policies. Mitton is a Vietnam correspondent for The Straits Times, *an English-language newspaper based in Singapore.*

As you read, consider the following questions:

1. Describe the subject matter of the two art exhibits that were closed down by the Communist Party's cultural commission.

2. How are artists and writers perceived by the regime, according to Mitton?

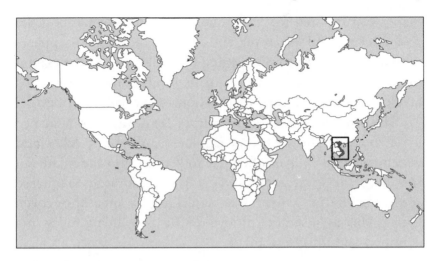

3. According to Dr. Le Bach Duong, director of Hanoi's Institute for Social Development Studies, what type of press reporting is not tolerated by government authorities?

The lounge of Hanoi's downtown Viet Art Centre is a great spot for discreet meetings away from the heat, noise and madding crowds of the city.

But a hubbub erupted there earlier this year [2007], and it reflected Hanoi's dilemma in trying to control information and the arts while integrating with the global community.

Exhibits Criticize Hanoi and Its Government

The gallery held a modernistic exhibition sponsored by Germany's Goethe Institute. All the displays came from Europe, except for a couple by local artists. It was the Vietnamese creations that caused a furore.

Artist Truong Tan's *Hidden Beauty* was a design installation in the shape of a giant diaper. He made it by sewing together hundreds of pockets designed like those used for the uniforms of Vietnamese traffic policemen. Said Mr Tan: 'My diaper can be used for a lifetime. It has many small pouches and pockets and whatever ends up inside them disappears permanently.' The crowds jostling excitedly around the exhibit did not need any explanation of its symbolism—it was a dig at Vietnamese policemen's reputation for pocketing bribes.

The other local exhibit, *Temple Of Love*, was a swan-shaped pedal boat of the type that can be seen on city lakes and which courting couples often use to get out into the middle of the lakes for some rare privacy. The elaborately lacquered specimen in the gallery was described by creator Nguyen Quang Huy as 'a symbol of love for all those living today in a cramped and dusty Hanoi'.

So you get the picture: One exhibit evoked the vulgarity of endemic police corruption and the other extolled amorous sanctuaries for urban lovers.

Ruling Communist Party Does Not Tolerate Dissenting Artists and Writers

When members of the ruling Communist Party's cultural commission attended the opening night, they were gob-smacked. A protest was swiftly registered, and the two exhibits were carted away.

Said Mr Tan: 'Vietnam is supposed to be getting more open, striving to catch up with the world. But the authority's actions were wild.'

The episode showed that the regime regards culture and information in much the same way it was in the former Soviet Union: Artists and writers are viewed with suspicion. Their creative tendencies are known to reflect dangerously independent thoughts and anti-establishment attitudes.

And that sort of thing does not sit well with a one-party regime that brooks no criticism.

In fact, as Mr Truong Tan Sang, a key member of the politburo, reiterated last month [August 2007], Vietnam's artistic community should reflect the nation's development and

Performance Art Defies Vietnam's Culture Police

In recent years, the genre has been steadily gaining ground. Because of its inherent mobility and fleeting nature—the artist needs few materials and can perform the impromptu work anywhere—Vietnamese artists have been using performance art to quietly push the boundaries of acceptable social and political commentaries while avoiding the censor's watchful eye. "As a form of expression, performance's ephemeral nature offers visibility to a wide audience but invisibility to the authorities," [says Vietnamese art expert and professor Nora Taylor].

Sonia Kolesnikov-Jessop, "Words Cannot Express;
In Vietnam, Performance Art Is Gaining Favor as a
Way to Push Boundaries While Evading Censorship,"
Newsweek *(International Edition), July 14, 2008.*

progress positively. It should not satirise the forces of law and order, nor extol decadent and lascivious behaviour.

Perhaps recalling the art exhibition fiasco, Mr Sang cautioned that Vietnam's integration with the global community will present major challenges for the media and the arts.

Global Integration Proves Challenging for Censors

However, it is not the nation's painters, poets and pressmen who will face the greatest challenges, but rather Vietnam's cultural gatekeepers themselves.

As it opens up and gets more involved in global affairs, Vietnam is witnessing not only an astonishing influx of foreign investments, expatriate businessmen and tourists, but also art exhibitions, theatre shows, movies, magazines and newspapers from around the world. As a result, its people are being exposed to a greater range of artistic and cultural expression than they ever were before.

It is a nightmare for the watchdogs and the censors. As one artistic display or media report is deemed inappropriate and expunged, another two pop up.

It is not the nation's painters, poets and pressmen who will face the greatest challenges, but rather Vietnam's cultural gatekeepers.

A Two-Pronged Strategy

In an attempt to stem the tide, punishments have been stiffened to create fear and thus promote self-censorship, while rewards have been boosted for artists and journalists who toe the party line.

Two recent incidents involving the media illustrate the two-pronged strategy.

While the Vietnamese press is all state-owned and heavily monitored, it has become slightly more forceful in recent years. No paper has pushed the envelope more than *Tuoi Tre* (Youth), a popular daily that occasionally exposes bureaucratic incompetence and misbehaviour. Of course, as it is owned by the Ho Chi Minh City Youth Union, itself an arm of the Vietnamese Communist Party, its exposures are always carefully vetted first. And it never directly attacks the regime or the party's involvement in business deals.

Said Dr Le Bach Duong, director of Hanoi's Institute for Social Development Studies: 'The authorities will allow newspapers to report most things, as long as they do not criticise the party or the one-party system.'

In the recent past, however, there have been intimations from *Tuoi Tre* that seemed to suggest it wanted to be allowed to do those things.

That was too much for the party's gatekeepers. So last month, the paper's two respected deputy editors, Mr Huynh Son Phuoc and Mr Quang Vinh, were dismissed. Concurrently, there were lashings of praise for editors and reporters who pleased the government. On Aug 28, the top national press award was given to *Quan Doi Nhan Dan*, the official army newspaper, for an article 'describing the insidious nature of hostile Western influences'.

The gatekeepers are still winning the battle, but they may end up losing the war.

Two other top prizes went to stories about the life of a factory hand and a television documentary about a metallurgy worker.

There were no prizes for exposures of police corruption or flirtatious behaviour by youths.

Clearly, the gatekeepers are still winning the battle, but they may end up losing the war.

Zimbabwe's President Attempts to Silence Dissent Staged in Political Satires

Robyn Dixon

In the following viewpoint, Robyn Dixon reports on Zimbabwe's thriving protest arts culture, which continues despite the feared Central Intelligence Organization's censorship through threats, arrests, and, at times, killings of dissenters. Dixon examines theater, specifically political satire, as a major outlet for creative criticism of Zimbabwe's problems. According to Dixon, play productions in Zimbabwe are frequently shut down if the material is interpreted as insulting to the government or able to rouse protest. Dixon explains that the danger of arrest has led to a growing underground theater movement, with events held in unconventional places and through unique approaches that are more difficult to censor. Dixon, a recipient of the Robert F. Kennedy Journalism Award in the International Print Category for her coverage of Zimbabwe in 2007, is the Los Angeles Times' *bureau chief in Johannesburg, South Africa.*

As you read, consider the following questions:

1. According to Dixon, actors Anthony Tongani and Silvanos Mudzvova were arrested and originally charged with "inciting the masses to revolt." What penalty does this statute carry?

Robyn Dixon, "In Zimbabwe's Theatre of Fear, Dissent Plays On," *Los Angeles Times*, November 19, 2007. Copyright 2007 Los Angeles Times. Reproduced by permission.

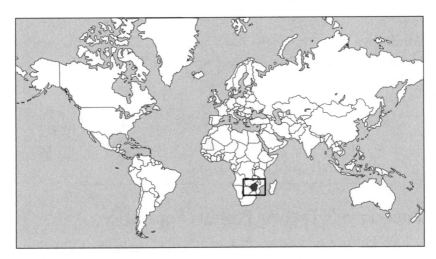

2. In what types of locations does the Invisible Theater appear?

3. How does Mudzvova explain the process of "hit-and-run theater"?

The stage was a small room in the Harare Central Police Station. The audience, about 20 bored policemen and plainclothes intelligence officers.

The two actors were shaking, not with stage fright but the real thing. Anthony Tongani stammered and forgot his lines. Silvanos Mudzvova was so afraid that he didn't dare make a mistake.

They stumbled to the end. Then they were ordered to start again.

And again.

They performed their political satire, *The Final Push*, twelve times in two days at the station, while police and officers from the feared Central Intelligence Organization [CIO] argued over what charges to press against the actors and fired questions about who had funded the show.

"The first time, the officer in charge was not there. When he came, he demanded his own performance. Then the superintendent came, and he demanded his own performance," Mudzvova said. "It got worse when the CIO came in. One of them was actually sleeping during the performance. Then he'd wake up and say, 'Are you through?'"

The political satire The Final Push *was performed twelve times in two days for police officers and officers from the Central Intelligence Organization.*

Zimbabwe's Theater Protests Repression

A rich culture of protest theater has sprung up in Zimbabwe, but artists are under increasing pressure from President Robert Mugabe's security forces as he crushes dissent. In recent years, most independent newspapers have been shut down, opposition parties have been infiltrated by CIO spies, and activists have been arrested, beaten and sometimes killed. The 2002 Public Order and Security Act bans political meetings of more than two people without police permission, outlaws statements that incite "public disorder" and makes it an offense to insult the president.

Mudzvova and Tongani were arrested at the premiere of *The Final Push* in late September. Tongani was arrested before he could take his final bow, and Mudzvova immediately after taking his.

Zimbabwe's underground arts culture is thriving, taking hard-hitting political messages to the masses.

The play, written by Mudzvova, is about the chairman of a building called Liberty House (a thinly disguised Mugabe) and his political challenger (presumed to be opposition leader Morgan Tsvangirai) trapped together in an elevator during a power failure. At one point, the two duke it out in a boxing match.

In Zimbabwe's repressive climate, artists and actors find creative ways to protest. People crowd into clubs to drink beer and laugh at stand-up comedy poking fun at Zimbabwe's problems. They turn out for the opening nights of political plays, even though police often raid theaters and close productions before the first lines are spoken.

Zimbabwe's underground arts culture is thriving, taking hard-hitting political messages to the masses in the crowded black townships, the engines of their cars running in case they need to make a quick escape from the authorities. Filmmakers recently secretly shot an underground movie based on a banned political play in Harare, the capital.

The two nights Mudzvova and Tongani spent in custody had elements of the kind of surreal political play in which they might perform. Police laughed in all the right places, especially when the chairman gets knocked out by his opponent. But the CIO men were outraged.

"The CIO guys tried to convince the police that we were actually talking about the president being knocked down," Mudzvova recounted in an interview the day after his release. "But the police did not see it in that way. To them it was just a simple, straightforward story.

"The police did not know what to do with us. But the CIO kept insisting that we be charged. The question was, with what?"

In the end, Mudzvova and Tongani were charged with inciting the masses to revolt, a statute that carries a 20-year penalty. Twice, police modified the charges, first to criminal nuisance, and then breach of the censorship laws.

Mudzvova says that with media freedom hobbled, it is up to artists to take a message of protest to Zimbabweans.

"Artists, like everybody else, fear for their lives. But the moment you have that fear, you won't get anywhere. People are saying, 'If you guys have that fear, where are we going to get the correct information from?'"

The night after their release, the two men were back on-stage in the small circular Theatre in the Park, modeled on an African hut, in Harare. But they modified the script to satisfy the CIO: The knockout in the boxing scene was gone. A day later, after debate with colleagues and actors, they restored the scene, without drawing further visits from the police.

An Unlikely Career

Bulawayo-based satirist Cont Mhlanga grew up in a village with no theatrical tradition. His father expected him to be a farmer. Mhlanga didn't intend to become an actor, because he didn't even know what it was.

Even today in Zimbabwe, the idea of a career in the theater is unthinkable for most people. It is seen as a last resort for beggars and failures, people incapable of producing something real to eat or sell.

He was introduced to theater by accident when a group wanted to hold a drama workshop in the hall where Mhlanga practiced karate. "I said, 'What is theater?'" But he joined in, got hooked and has been writing political satire since Zimbabwe won independence from Britain in 1980.

Stepping into Mhlanga's cluttered Bulawayo office is like visiting the inside of an inspired but chaotic mind, crammed with yard-high stacks of books, yellowing newspapers and scripts, drafts of his latest protest letter to the government, and pieces of old broken, unidentifiable equipment, with a sleek laptop basking happily in the middle of it all.

Wiry, with piercing eyes, he speaks in a tumble of words. He does not look old but declines to give his age, shrugging scornfully at the question.

"Everyone around here calls me Grandfather," he said dryly.

His plays are so bluntly political that he and his actors frequently get into trouble.

Artistic Expression Is a Human Need

Art is not a weak or irrelevant force: when everything is closed and the economy is in ruins, with mob brutality becoming the rule, there is immense release through the arts. The ancient Greeks knew it; they called it catharsis. Our need for such release is innate in human nature.

Paul Brickhill, "Arts in Zimbabwe:
A Movement Fighting Oppression," Art and Design Blog,
The Guardian, July 3, 2008. www.guardian.co.uk.

In May, the officer-in-charge at Bulawayo Central Police Station went through Mhlanga's play about AIDS, *Everyday Soldier*, deleting lines with a red pen, offended because one character disappears as part of the plot.

"He said, 'You can't have this because you are implying that people disappear in Zimbabwe.' I said, 'I'm not going to remove the lines. It will play as it is.' He said, 'It will not play as it is. I'll close it down.'"

He did prevent public presentation of the play, but Mhlanga found a way around it: "We started to run the play for closed audiences. We just make sure there are no police in the audience."

Mhlanga's latest play, *The Good President*, inspired by beatings and arrests of opposition members in March, was shut down on opening night in June, and riot police surrounded the theater for a week to prevent the actors from staging the play.

To evade arrest or censorship, artists run underground projects. Mhlanga invented what he calls Invisible Theater in bars, trains and the commuter minibuses called taxis.

In Invisible Theater, several actors plant themselves in a group and improvise a conversation.

"People don't know they're actors. The dialogue might be: 'This government is terrible. Look at those kids in the street. They should be in school but they're carrying water.' Then another actor will say, 'Don't start with that. You'll get us all beaten. There are CIO guys everywhere.' Then a third actor will say, 'The way we're living in this country is more than a beating.'

"The thing [Invisible Theater actors] are challenging is fear, because we know that people are afraid of discussing these things in public."

"Then other people will join in," he said, referring to the unsuspecting people around them. "The actors will keep directing the conversation, and the moment they think they've made a point, they will get off the taxi and get onto another one.

"The thing we are challenging is fear, because we know that people are afraid of discussing these things in public."

"Hit-and-Run" Shows

In Harare, a theater organization named Savanna Trust does "hit-and-run" street performances in volatile areas such as Mashonaland West, where actors risk arrest by police or violence from ruling party thugs.

They're designed to reach people in poor, crowded neighborhoods who otherwise would never see theater. The performance must be quick, sharp and funny, and the actors ready for a quick getaway.

"When you do hit-and-run theater, you beat drums and the people gather. You have a car there with the motor running," Mudzvova said. "Your heart is beating very fast. You are full of fear that you are going to be arrested at any minute.

You know the exact message that you want to give. You make sure the people get the message in the shortest time. As soon as you see that people are getting the message, you disappear.

"Afterwards the actors go, 'Phew! That was extreme!'

"We escaped by a whisker in Bindura," he said, referring to a stronghold of the ruling party. "We only escaped because the car we had was far more powerful than the car the police had."

A Film Made on the Sly

Mudzvova is not the only one producing controversial material. The low-budget underground film *Super Patriots and Morons*, produced by British-trained Zimbabwean actor Daves Guzha, was filmed secretly over nine days in Harare. It includes real scenes of Harare street life, bread queues and crushing poverty.

Filming without permission is banned in Zimbabwe, and the filmmakers, questioned by police while they were working, were lucky to escape arrest.

The film's portrait of an isolated, paranoid president haunted by dreams of a bloody hangman's rope is unlikely to hit cinema screens in Zimbabwe. The best its makers can hope for is mass production of DVDs that could be distributed free. But there is no money for that, so the film's future is unclear.

"It's up to us as citizens of this country to demand our freedoms if we feel they are being curtailed and to assert ourselves," [film director Tawanda Gunda Mumpengo] said, "because no one will do it for us."

The director, Tawanda Gunda Mumpengo, is critical of what he sees as self-censorship by artists terrified of arrest and violence.

"It's up to us as citizens of this country to demand our freedoms if we feel they are being curtailed and to assert ourselves," he said, "because no one will do it for us."

In his jumbled office, Mhlanga gestured at the mountains of papers around him, the fruit of 27 years of labor. "No one will shut me up," he said. "There's only one option to shut me up and that's to kill me. But they can't kill what I stand for."

North Korea's Communist Regime Strictly Controls Art and Archaeology

Mitch Davis

In the following viewpoint, Mitch Davis reports on British museum curator Jane Portal's explanation of North Korea's art censorship, during a lecture at Dartmouth College. Portal, curator of the museum's China and Korea collections, claims that the subject matter of North Korean artwork is controlled by the Communist regime to promote socialist ideals, celebrate Korean myth, and reflect on the country's natural beauty. Portal recognizes that besides contemporary visual artwork, the state also controls archeology by sometimes making false claims as to what the artifacts and their origins are. Davis wrote this article as a staff member of The Dartmouth, *Dartmouth College's newspaper.*

As you read, consider the following questions:

1. According to Portal, since North Korea's formation in 1948, what artistic tradition has been influential?
2. According to Portal, whose image is frequently used in North Korean art?
3. What does Portal describe as the government's purpose in moving a well-known Buddhist temple?

Mitch Davis, "Speaker Probes North Korea's Art Censorship," *The Dartmouth*, April 29, 2008. http://thedartmouth.com. Copyright 2008 by The Dartmouth, Inc. All rights reserved. Reproduced by permission.

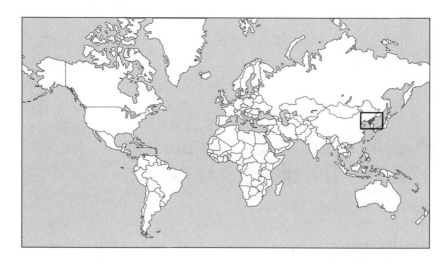

North Korea's Communist regime controls the work of native artists to achieve state ends, Jane Portal, a curator of the British Museum, stated in a lecture Monday [April 2008] in Carson Hall. During visits to North Korea in 2001 and 2002, Portal found art that revealed a cultural sphere strictly controlled and restricted by the state.

"This is not art, basically," Portal said. "It's propaganda . . . Some of it's technically very good, it's just the subject matter is limited."

Portal is curator of the British Museum's China and Korea collections. She traveled to North Korea to look for art for the museum's collection.

State-Controlled Art

Since Kim Il Sung took power, forming North Korea in 1948, the country's limited contact with other cultures has included the importation of socialist art, primarily from China and the former Soviet Union, Portal said. This art primarily features the glorification of soldiers and laborers, according to Portal. Any visual art that deviates from standards of socialist realism or subjects of traditional Korean art, such as landscapes, is prohibited by the government, she said.

North Korea Is the World's Most Censored Country

North Korea has wedded the traditional Confucian ideal of social order to the Stalinist [former Soviet dictator Joseph Stalin] model of an authoritarian Communist state to create the world's deepest information void. All domestic radio, television, and newspapers are controlled by the government. Radio and television receivers are locked to government-specified frequencies. Content is supplied almost entirely by the official Korean Central News Agency (KCNA). It serves up a daily diet of fawning coverage of "Dear Leader" Kim Jong-Il and his official engagements. The country's grinding poverty or famines are never mentioned. Only small numbers of foreign journalists are allowed limited access each year, and they must be accompanied by "minders" wherever they go.

After a deadly munitions train explosion in April 2004 in Ryongchon near the Chinese border, KCNA reported that citizens displayed the "spirit of guarding the leader with their very lives" by rushing into burning buildings to save portraits of Kim "before searching for their family members or saving their household goods." The international press, meanwhile, was barred from the scene, where more than 150 died and thousands were injured.

Committee to Protect Journalists, "North Korea Tops CPJ List '10 Most Censored Countries,'" May 2, 2006. www.cpj.org.

Kim is a recurring figure in North Korean art, a genre Portal calls "Kim cult" art. Kim has been the subject of pictures, songs, poems, stories and even a species of orchid named "kimilsungia" in his honor, according to Portal. Kim's image, frequently surrounded by children, is painted on many multistory murals on the sides of new buildings, she said.

"It's probably the case that Kim Il Sung has had more buildings named after him during his life than any other leader in modern history," Portal said. "Kim was associated with benevolence. He came to be regarded as a kind of Father Christmas or Santa Claus."

Any visual art that deviates from standards of socialist realism or subjects of traditional Korean art . . . is prohibited by the government.

North Korean Archaeology Misrepresented for Political Means

The state's control of art parallels its influence on the work of North Korean archaeologists, Portal said. For example, the government falsely claimed that the remains of two bodies uncovered by archaeologists were the bodies of Korea's mythical founder, Dangun, and his wife. Officials constructed a mausoleum to commemorate the site where the bodies were found, Portal said.

Portal referred to the mausoleum as "rather like a dramatic but historically incorrect film set" appropriated by the government to enhance public support of the state. The history of other monuments has been revised by the state as well, she said, such as a Buddhist temple constructed by a major past figure in Korean history, which the government moved to a more central location during North Korea's reconstruction. The purpose of the move was to increase state legitimacy and historical power in the eyes of North Koreans.

"A lot of time and money has been put into this reconstructed Buddhist temple," Portal said. "It was renovated and relocated for political reasons."

In other cases, sites generally regarded by archaeologists as Chinese settlements have either been ignored or treated as if they were Korean sites, she said. Chinese objects discovered by archaeologists, such as jade figures, have been studied as if they were Korean subjects, she said.

Gradual Global Integration Could Eventually Increase Acceptance of Artistic Expression

Such cultural isolation is part of North Korea's larger policy of "Juche," or self-reliance, according to Portal. The state has made an effort to focus the North Korean people entirely inward, Portal said, and has trained them to believe that North Korea is a form of paradise. As a result, the country has only recently begun to open to the outside world, in response to the democratization of a number of other former Communist regimes, according to Portal.

"I think that there is a problem with money and lack of resources and lack of equipment," Portal said. "Korea's just stuck in this kind of time warp, and nothing's happening. . . . There is a gradual opening up, but it is very, very gradual."

Portal aims to document the current condition of North Korea, which she has attempted to do by bringing North Korean art to Britain for preservation, she said.

"The regime is going to change at some time, we know not when," she said. "It needs collecting and recording. Make what you will of it."

Periodical Bibliography

The following articles have been selected to supplement the diverse views presented in this chapter.

Leila Cobo — "Chavez the Censor: It May Be Hip to Praise Hugo, but He's Silencing a Singer," *Billboard*, vol. 120, no. 8, February 23, 2008.

Dominio Cooke — "An Insidious Form of Censorship," *Spectator*, October 11, 2008.

The Evening Standard (London) — "Prudish America Censors Gilbert and George Show," October 1, 2008.

Howard W. French — "Censored in Shanghai, but a Hit in Hong Kong," *International Herald Tribune*, December 19, 2007.

Sonia Kolesnikov-Jessop — "Words Cannot Express," *Newsweek International*, July 14, 2008.

Anna Quindlen — "Write and Wrong," *Newsweek*, July 21, 2008.

Diane Steinle — "Council Insists It Will Know and Ban 'Bad' Art," *St. Petersburg Times* (St. Petersburg, FL), December 7, 2008.

Time — "When Cultures Collide: Observers Around the World Tell *Time* How They View the Cartoons—and the Controversy They've Sparked," February 13, 2006.

The Times (London) — "Censors Abandon Nation's 40-year Ban on Bollywood," January 23, 2006.

GLOBALVIEWPOINTS

CHAPTER 3

Internet Censorship

Palestinian Leaders Block Access to Pornographic Web Sites in Gaza

Kuwait Times

In the following viewpoint from Agence France-Presse, published in the Kuwait Times, *the author explains that Hamas, the militant organization that won the 2006 general legislative elections in Palestine, has installed a filter to block Internet pornography in Gaza. The author points out that the stated objective of this filter is to "protect morality." According to the author, the filter has affected Internet speed, leading to slower business at Internet cafes. The author notes that pornography has not been erased from Gaza computer screens altogether, since software can be obtained online to bypass the filter. Based in Kuwait and founded in September 1961 by Yousuf Saleh Alyan,* Kuwait Times *was the first English-language daily newspaper in the Persian Gulf region. Agence France-Presse, based in Paris, France, is the oldest news service agency in existence.*

As you read, consider the following questions:

1. According to the author, what often occurred when Internet cafe owners attempted to prevent access to pornography Web sites before the filter was installed?

2. According to a Hamas memorandum, what is the mission behind installing this filter?

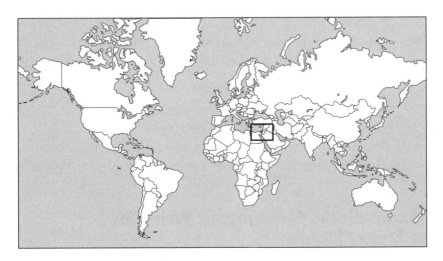

3. What conflict has PalTel, the Palestinian telecommunications company, faced concerning blocking pornography from all high-speed Internet subscribers?

First it went after drug dealers, then booze and car theft. Now the Palestinian movement Hamas, which seized power in Gaza a year ago, is taking on another challenge to its self-styled Islamist rule—Internet pornography. "A couple of weeks ago Hamas installed a filter to prevent people from accessing such pages on the net," said Ali Sarayfi, who runs an Internet cafe in the university area of Gaza City.

Inside the cafe dozens of young people are glued to computer monitors, surfing the Internet and enjoying one of their last remaining links to the world outside the fenced-off territory. Since Hamas took over the Gaza Strip on June 15 last year [2007] after routing forces loyal to the secular Palestinian president Mahmud Abbas, Israel has sealed the impoverished territory off from all but limited humanitarian aid.

With the economy teetering on the edge of collapse and the vast majority of Gaza's residents out of work, the Internet cafes are one of the last affordable recreational outlets available to the territory's 1.5 million people. Huddled in cubicles and sporting nervous smiles, their attention is focused on on-line role-playing games such as Counter Strike. Others check to see if they have any messages on the social networking site Facebook.

[Internet filters were installed] "*to protect the sons of the Palestinian people and reinforce morale and Palestinian national concepts.*"

Hamas Blocks Pornographic Web Sites to Protect Morale

"Before, anyone could gain access to sites with sexual content, and some people even came here to do just that," said Sarayfi. "But today that's all finished, and it's better that way." In the past when some Internet cafe owners tried to prevent access to certain sites, "they were threatened. People in powerful Gaza families told them the windows in their shops would be broken," he added.

The current porn crackdown by Hamas was foreshadowed last year with the firebombing of several Gaza City establishments. Most of the attacks were claimed by an extremist group calling itself "The Swords of Truth" that said Internet cafes offered young Palestinians access to pornographic Web sites.

In mid-May, the Hamas-run authorities in Gaza signed an accord with PalTel, the Palestinian telecommunications company, "to protect the sons of the Palestinian people and reinforce morale and Palestinian national concepts," according to the text of a memorandum obtained by AFP [Agence France-Presse]. Under the terms of the agreement, PalTel—the sole Internet service provider or ISP in the Palestinian territories—filters out addresses to pornographic websites.

"Palestinian society suffers because of such immoral sites. We have therefore taken the decision to protect morality, and this remains our policy," Hamas telecommunications minister

Australia's Plan to Block Explicit Online Materials Sparks Controversy

The plan . . . has two tiers. A mandatory filter would block sites on an existing blacklist determined by the Australian Communications Media Authority. An optional filter would block adult content.

The latter could use keywords to determine which sites to block, a technology that critics say is problematic.

"Filtering technology is not capable of realizing that when we say breasts we're talking about breast cancer, or when we type in sex we may be looking for sexual education," [said Gordie Guy, spokesman for Electronic Frontiers Australia, an Internet advocacy organization]. "The filter will accidentally block things it's not meant to block."

USA Today, *"Uproar in Australia over Plan to Block Websites,"*
December 26, 2008. www.ustoday.com.

Yussef Al-Mansi told AFP. "After a year of talks with PalTel we've finally succeeding in blocking (pornographic sites)," he added. Now Internet users are complaining—not because porn sites are no longer available but because the mechanism blocking them has slowed connections to a crawl.

The Challenges and Consequences of Filtering Internet Content

Legal adviser Sharhabil Al-Zaim of PalTel management said Hamas "asked that access to these sites be blocked for all high-speed subscribers, but PalTel cannot install filters governing more than 5,000 subscribers." Such capacity is minuscule, given the rising number of ADSL [asymmetric digital subscriber line] subscribers in the Gaza Strip that currently stands at more than 50,000, according to one PalTel source.

"For the past two weeks the net has been really slow. People don't want to have to wait two hours just to open a page," said Mohammed, who runs an Internet cafe near the Islamic University of Gaza. "It's all very well blocking porn sites, but they don't know how to do it properly and they're destroying our business," he added. "It only creates problems for companies and for students who really need the Internet."

Mansi, the Hamas minister, said that PalTel "has begun to resolve the problem—connections are back up to 90 percent or near normal speed." His claim would be disputed by anyone in Gaza with access to an Internet-linked computer. They can check the speed of a connection—or lack of it—for themselves.

But as always, savvy computer users have come up with a "workaround" or temporary fix to the problem—downloadable software that allows the blocking filter to be bypassed. Their ingenuity insures that even if Gaza continues to suffer from shortages of fuel, electricity, and basic goods, no siege will keep out the pornography that so troubles its hardline Islamist rulers.

Thailand and Turkey Ban YouTube Web Site

The Economist

In the following selection from The Economist, *the author reports on Thailand's and Turkey's decisions to ban the video-sharing Web site YouTube, provoked by video clips that the countries' leaders felt were insulting their nations. According to the author, plans by both countries to ban the Web site led to more exposure and attention to the clips, which were viewed through other providers after the bans. While YouTube would not remove the clip found insulting to the Thai monarch, the company did remove the one that Turkey deemed insulting due to its use of hate speech. After this article's publication, in August 2007, Thailand overturned its YouTube ban, following up with a filter system that blocks offensive material.* The Economist *is a London and New York-based news and features magazine focusing on international economics, business, and policy. The publication traditionally omits author bylines.*

As you read, consider the following questions:

1. According to the author, what was the content of the video clip that provoked Thailand's YouTube ban?
2. How does the author describe the video clip that provoked Turkey to ban YouTube?

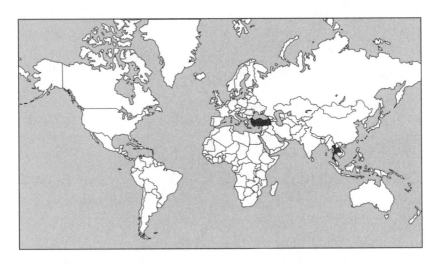

3. Though YouTube claims to avoid censoring the Web site's content as much as possible, what does it block, according to the author?

At first sight, anyway, it seems like one more case of a clumsy, authoritarian government being wrong-footed by nimble creatures from cyberspace who acknowledge no borders and can leap effortlessly over almost any obstacle. YouTube, the Web site that dominates the market in user-generated, online videos (or in plain language, a place where almost anybody can post a film about almost anything) has been blocked by Thailand's military-backed government. The ban was imposed in a fit of indignation over a 44-second clip that mocked the country's monarch. It was a crude bit of work, showing King Bhumibol Adulyadej with feet over his face and mouth, an image certain to offend Thai Buddhists.

Thailand's Case

Given that last year's [2006] coup in Bangkok was presented as an action carried out in the name of the king, Thailand's rulers have a big stake in the sovereign's prestige. Hence their demand to the California-based site (bought last year by

Google for $1.65 billion) to scrap the offensive material; and their decision, when faced with YouTube's refusal, to block access to the whole site. "When they decide to withdraw the clip, we'll withdraw the ban," snapped Sitthichai Pookaiyaudom, the communications minister.

But if the aim was to shore up the law against *lèse-majesté* [a crime against a monarch] (under which a Swiss man was jailed for ten years for defacing portraits of the king and queen, only to be pardoned this week [April 2007]), it backfired. Within days of the site being blocked in Thailand, the clip was seen 16,000 times by people round the world. Then the clip was removed (by its maker) but many others, also insulting to the king, were posted.

YouTube commented that the site had not broken American law, and pointed out that it was replete with negative images of other leaders, like George Bush. Some Thais reacted peevishly; they pointed out that YouTube's parent, Google, does co-operate with China's authorities as they block subversive material from the Chinese version of the search engine. But quite a lot of Thais blamed the government for turning an obscure bit of nonsense into a global free-speech issue. And Bangkok's youngsters, as Internet-savvy as their counterparts all over the world, rushed to view the anti-royalist footage on alternative providers.

Within days of [YouTube] being blocked in Thailand, the [offending video] clip was seen 16,000 times by people round the world.

Turkey's Case

To those who follow the politics of the Internet, the story instantly recalled one that unfolded in Turkey a few weeks earlier. An Istanbul court told the newly privatised service provider, Turk Telekom, to ban access to YouTube after it carried

Blocking of Social Content on the Internet

Thailand and Turkey are just two of many countries worldwide that have been affected by the blocking of social Internet sites. In 2008, Pakistan, Iran, and Saudi Arabia also blocked YouTube. Other countries, as this map shows, have blocked access to online social content to varying degrees.

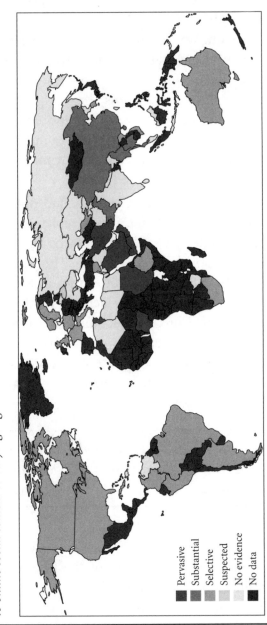

Pervasive
Substantial
Selective
Suspected
No evidence
No data

TAKEN FROM: "Blocked YouTube," Economist.com, February 27, 2008. http://media.economist.com.

a video-clip, submitted by a user with a Greek-sounding name, portraying Turkey's state founder, Kemal Ataturk, as a boastful, grotesque-looking homosexual. The judge's move followed a barrage of e-mails (220,000 in a single day) that expressed outrage over the desecration of a revered statesman. But within minutes of the ban, YouTube fans realised they could still gain access to the site through other providers—and just as in Thailand, a mood of indignation over insults to a sacrosanct figure gave way (among some citizens) to a sense of anger that the authorities had used sledgehammer tactics. "The ban shows that Turkey has not caught up with the reality of modern technology," said Cihat Selim, an Internet pundit. The Turkish tale, at least, has a happy-ish ending; the ban was lifted after the controversial clip was removed.

YouTube's Policies Include Minimal Editing of Content

YouTube says it interferes as little as possible with the material on the site; but it does block "hate speech" and material that is offensive on grounds of race, religion or sexual orientation, as well as extreme violence and explicit sex. (The latter rule was cited in Brazil earlier this year when film of a model cavorting with her boyfriend led to a block for several days—followed by a plethora of ironic imitations.)

One of Google's regulation wonks, Andrew McLaughlin, said the firm obeys the law wherever it operates—but given that it has no office or staff in Thailand, it is not a Thai service or subject to Thai law.

> *Sites like YouTube face huge problems if they wield editorial power, and huge problems if they don't.*

Tim Wu, an Internet expert at Columbia Law School in New York, says sites like YouTube face huge problems if they wield editorial power, and huge problems if they don't. Wherever possible, they will stick to the latter course, because as soon as they make any decision about editorial issues they will risk accepting responsibility for the site's whole contents. At the moment, says Mr Wu, sites can say they are no more responsible for the way their space is used than telephone companies are for crimes discussed by users of their lines. The sites would love to keep things as simple as that, but in a world of clashing ideas about the limits of decency, blasphemy and dissent, that is going to be very hard.

Nor will all government pressure on sites and providers have to do with high politics or ancient traditions. Britain's education minister, Alan Johnson, said this week that Internet sites had a "moral obligation" to stop pupils posting videos that demean teachers or other children.

China Hires Internet Commentators to Stifle Dissent

Jonathan Watts

In the following viewpoint, Jonathan Watts reports on China's heightened Internet censorship, enabled by an Internet commentator team assembled by Chinese authorities. These commentators are trained to anonymously orchestrate neutral online discussions as well as veer users away from politically sensitive subjects on public message boards. Watts relates that prior to the organization of Internet commentator teams, online censorship took the form of an Internet police force working to monitor and censor Web communication, deleting messages deemed dissenting or controversial. According to Watts, critics of the newer form of censorship, the Internet commentators, argue that the "anonymous spread of government propaganda" is an "abuse of power." Watts is The Guardian's *east Asia correspondent.*

As you read, consider the following questions:

1. According to Watts, what were the major Internet-based protests that provoked China's heightened censorship using Internet commentators?

2. What is the summarized mission of the Internet commentators as described by Watts?

3. According to Watts, approximately how many people made up China's Internet police force as of 2005?

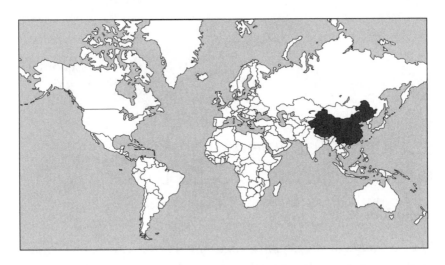

China's Communist authorities have intensified their campaign against the party's biggest potential enemy—the Internet—with the recruitment of a growing army of secret Web commentators, sophisticated new monitoring software and a warning that all bloggers and bulletin board operators must register with the government or be closed down and fined.

The escalation of the government's effort to neutralize critical online opinion comes after a series of large anti-Japanese, anti-pollution and anti-corruption protests, many of which were organised or publicised using instant messaging services, chatrooms and text messages.

With the number of users forecast to rise above 100 million this year, access to the Web is spreading beyond China's well-rewarded middle class and into the more disgruntled factory and farming communities, where young migrant workers are teaching their families about Internet cafes.

In response, the propaganda departments of provincial and municipal governments have recently been instructed to build teams of Internet commentators, whose job is to guide discussion on public bulletin boards away from politically sensitive topics by posting opinions anonymously or under false names.

Although advertisements are supposed to have been placed in-house, many details about the part-time political pacifiers have emerged in the domestic media. According to the *Southern Weekend* newspaper, a team of about 20 commentators has been operating in the city of Suqian, in Jiangsu province, since April.

Access to the Web is spreading beyond China's well-rewarded middle class and into the more disgruntled factory and farming communities.

"In the information age and the Internet age, the most important and critical mission in front of us is how to seize the initiative on Internet opinion and how to seize the high point of Internet opinion," the paper quoted the deputy director of the local propaganda department, Zhang Fenglin, as saying.

Applicants for the job—mostly drawn from the propaganda and police departments—were told they had to understand government policies, know political theory, be politically reliable and understand Internet technology. Successful candidates have been offered classes in Marxist theory, propaganda techniques and updates on the development of the Internet around the world.

A summary of objectives declared that commentators should "be proactive in developing discussion, increase control, accentuate the good, avoid the bad, and use Internet debate to our advantage."

Reports that at least two other localities have recruited similar teams suggest the strategy is being encouraged by the central government. Few will admit to the practice, but Nanjing officials said the city was hiring 20 online commentators from the ranks of its existing employees.

"They don't need to give up their current jobs because it is not full time. All they need to do is spend some time every

China Has the Most Sophisticated Internet Censoring Operations in the World

China's Internet filtering regime is the most sophisticated effort of its kind in the world. . . . It comprises multiple levels of legal regulation and technical control. It involves numerous state agencies and thousands of public and private personnel. It censors content transmitted through multiple methods, including Web pages, Web logs, on-line discussion forums, university bulletin board systems, and e-mail messages. Our testing found efforts to prevent access to a wide range of sensitive materials, from pornography to religious material to political dissent. ONI [OpenNet Initiative] sought to determine the degree to which China filters sites on topics that the Chinese government finds sensitive, and found that the state does so extensively. Chinese citizens seeking access to Web sites containing content related to Taiwanese and Tibetan independence, Falun Gong, the Dalai Lama, the Tiananmen Square incident, opposition political parties, or a variety of anti-Communist movements will frequently find themselves blocked. Despite conventional wisdom, though, ONI found that most major American media sites, such as CNN, MSNBC, and ABC, are generally available in China (though the BBC remains blocked). Moreover, most sites we tested in our global list's human rights and anonymizer categories are accessible as well. . . . [O]ur research documents a system that imposes strong controls on its citizens' ability to view and to publish Internet content.

OpenNet Initiative, "Internet Filtering in China in 2004–2005:
A Country Study," April 14, 2005. http://opennet.net.

day monitoring Internet discussion," said a member of the propaganda department. "There are commentators like this all over the country. Until now we haven't had detailed instructions about how it works. So nothing is clear yet."

Although the existence of an Internet police force—estimated at more than 30,000—has been known for some time, attention has previously focused on their work as censors and monitors. Countless critical comments appear on bulletin boards of major portals such as Sohu and Sina only to be erased minutes, or sometimes just seconds, later. In the most recent case, all postings that blamed corrupt local officials or slow-moving police for the deaths of 88 children in floods last Friday were removed almost as soon as they appeared.

But the task of covertly guiding opinion—as in Suqian—has proved controversial for different reasons. "I think Suqian's practice is not proper," said Zhan Jiang, dean of journalism at China Youth University for Political Sciences. "If officials want to guide public opinion they should publish an editorial in the *People's Daily* under their own names. It is very wrong to anonymously spread government propaganda. Online commentary is a kind of abuse of power."

China's leading bloggers were equally scathing. "The government's tactics are too funny. They are actually hiring staff to curse online," said Liu Di, who was arrested last year for comments she posted under her Internet moniker Iron Mouse. "But it also shows that the government can find no better way to deal with netizens' discussion. Compared to other media in China, the Internet is still the most free. It is powerful among young people no matter whether they are chatting online or playing games. It will be difficult for the government to control."

Iranian Bloggers Face Harassment

Lara Sukhtian

In the following viewpoint, Lara Sukhtian describes the Iranian government's harassment of what it perceives as dissenting and "immoral" Internet bloggers. Sukhtian explains that other forms of media such as newspapers, television, and radio have been greatly censored for some time under the Islamic republic, leaving the Internet as one of the last outlets for freedom of expression. However, the government is increasingly coming down on the blogging community, attempting to restrict not just political debate but also discussions of social issues. According to Sukhtian, this Iranian Weblog community has grown enormously since its introduction in 2001, making it a challenge for the government to control. Sukhtian writes for the Associated Press, an international newswire service.

As you read, consider the following questions:

1. According to Sukhtian, the Iranian government has the second most well-equipped Internet censoring operation behind what country?

2. Describe one case in which an Iranian political blogger was accused by the government, according to Sukhtian.

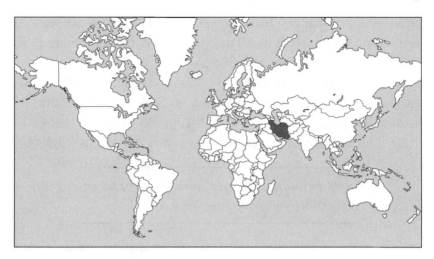

3. Sukhtian recognizes that though the Iranian government highly censors blogs, it does not want to ban them. Why is this, according to blogger Farid Pouya?

On his last visit to Iran, Canadian-based blogger Hossein Derakhshan was detained and interrogated, then forced to sign a letter of apology for his blog writings before being allowed to leave the country.

Compared to others, Derakhshan is lucky.

Dozens of Iranian bloggers over the last two years have faced harassment by the government, been arrested for voicing opposing views, and fled the country in fear of prosecution.

In the conservative Islamic Republic, where the government has vast control over newspapers and the airwaves, Weblogs are one of the last bastions of free expression, where people can speak openly about everything from sex to the nuclear controversy.

But increasingly, they are coming under threat of censorship.

The Iranian blogging community, known as Weblogistan, is relatively new. It sprang to life in 2001 after hardliners—fighting back against a reformist president—shut down more than 100 newspapers and magazines and detained writers. At the time, Derakhshan posted instructions on the Internet in Farsi on how to set up a Weblog.

Since then, the community has grown dramatically. Although exact figures are unknown, experts estimate there are somewhere between 70,000 and 100,000 active Weblogs in Iran. The vast majority are in Farsi but a few are in English.

... experts estimate there are somewhere between 70,000 and 100,000 active Weblogs in Iran.

Overall, the percentage of Iranians now blogging is "gigantic," said Curt Hopkins, director of an online group called the Committee to Protect Bloggers, who lives in Seattle, Wash.

"They are a talking people, very intellectual, social, and have a lot to say. And they are up against a small group (in the government) that are trying to shut everyone up," said Hopkins.

U.S. Software Aids Government

To bolster its campaign, the Iranian government has one of the most extensive and sophisticated operations to censor and filter Internet content of any country in the world—second only to China, Hopkins said.

It also is one of a growing number of Mideast countries that rely on U.S. commercial software to do the filtering, according to a 2004 study by a group called the OpenNet Initiative. The software that Iran uses blocks both internationally hosted sites in English and local sites in Farsi, the study found.

The filtering process is backed by laws that force individuals who subscribe to Internet service providers to sign a promise not to access non-Islamic sites. The same laws also force ISPs to install filtering mechanisms.

The filtering "is systematically getting worse," said Derakhshan.

Online Discussions of Social Issues Are as Taboo as Political Debates

But is the government threatened because the tens of thousands of Iranian blogs are all throwing insults at it, or calling for revolution? Not quite.

The debates on Iranian Weblogs are rarely political. The most common issues are cultural, social and sexual. Blogs also are a good place to chat in a society where young men and women cannot openly date. There are blogs that discuss women's issues, and ones that deal with art and photography.

"I am very careful. Every blogger in Iran who writes in his/her name must be careful. I know the red lines and I never go beyond them."

But in Iran, activists say all debates are equally perceived as a threat by the authorities. Bloggers living in Iran understand that better than anyone else.

"I am very careful. Every blogger in Iran who writes in his/her name must be careful. I know the red lines and I never go beyond them," said Parastoo Dokouhaki, 25, who runs one of Iran's most popular blogs, www.parastood.com. "And these days, the red lines are getting tighter."

Dokouhaki doesn't directly write about politics. She sticks mostly to social issues, but in Iran, that is also a taboo subject.

"I write about the social consequences of government decisions and they don't like it, because they can't control it," said Dokouhaki.

The Dangers of Online Political Discussion

Outright political bloggers have an even tougher time.

Hanif Mazroui was arrested in 1994 and charged with acting against the Islamic system through his writings. He was jailed for 66 days and then acquitted.

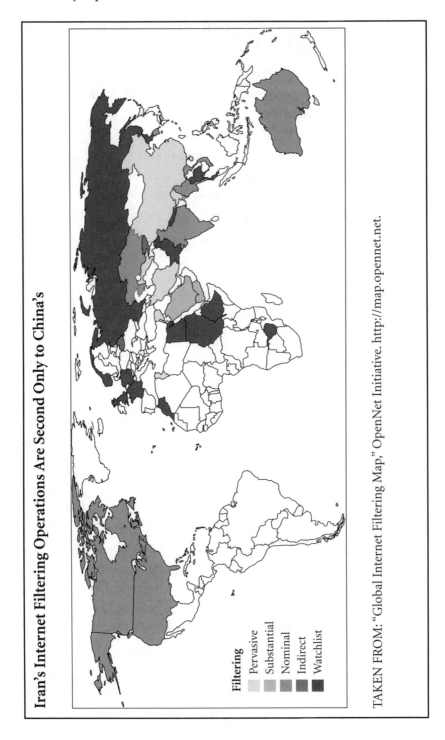

Iran's Internet Filtering Operations Are Second Only to China's

Filtering
Pervasive
Substantial
Nominal
Indirect
Watchlist

TAKEN FROM: "Global Internet Filtering Map," OpenNet Initiative. http://map.opennet.net.

"It's normal for authorities to summon and threaten blog-gers," said Mazroui. The government continued to harass him and three months ago, he was summoned once again by the authorities and told never to write about the nuclear issue. Soon after his release, he shut down his Weblog.

"They kept pressuring me," he said.

Arash Sigarchi, an Iranian journalist and blogger, was arrested and charged with insulting the country's leader, collaborating with the enemy, writing propaganda against the Islamic state and encouraging people to jeopardize national security.

"It's normal for authorities to summon and threaten bloggers."

He had been in jail for 60 days when he was sentenced to 14 years in jail. He appealed the decision and was released on bail. But though his sentence has been reduced to three years, he still faces charges of insulting the leader and writing propaganda.

Another, Mojtaba Saminejad, has been in prison since February 2005. He was first arrested in November 2004 for speaking out against the arrest of three colleagues. According to the Committee to Protect Bloggers, Saminejad's Web site was hacked into by people linked to the Iranian Hezbollah movement.

After his release, he relaunched his blog at a new address, which led to his second arrest in February 2005. He was sentenced to two years in prison, and then given an extra 10 months for inciting "immorality."

The Government Wants to Utilize Blogging to Its Advantage

Despite the crackdown, most Iranian bloggers say the government is not interested in eliminating the blogging trend altogether.

Instead, they believe authorities understand its power and want to use it to further their own goals.

Farid Pouya, a Belgian-based Iranian blogger who writes at webgardesh.blogspot.com, notes the government has just launched a competition for the best four blogs. The subjects: the Islamic revolution and the Koran.

"The government has observed carefully and learned that blogs are important . . . and they want to capitalize on that," she said. "They want to lead the movement, they want to control it."

The European Union Wants to Block Internet Searches for Bomb Recipes

David Charter and Jonathan Richards

In the following viewpoint, David Charter and Jonathan Richards report on the European Union's decision to criminalize the publication of bomb-making instructions on the Internet as a component of anti-terrorist proposals. According to a senior European Union official, criticisms that this decision violates freedom of expression will not be taken into account because such material could be used to aid terrorists. Charter and Richards explain that the proposal makes Internet service providers (ISPs) responsible for filtering out international Web sites that include bomb-making instructions or they will face legal consequences. The Internet Service Providers' Association (ISPA) claims that ISPs should not be criminalized for such Internet-published material because they are information carriers rather than editors. David Charter, a Europe correspondent, and Jonathan Richards write for The Times, *a London-based newspaper.*

As you read, consider the following questions:

1. According to Charter and Richards, what two bomb-related instances encouraged the decision to outlaw on-line bomb-making instructions?

David Charter and Jonathan Richards, "Website Bomb-Making Lessons to Be Outlawed Across Europe," *The Times* (London), July 4, 2007. Copyright 2007 Times Newspapers Ltd. Reproduced by permission.

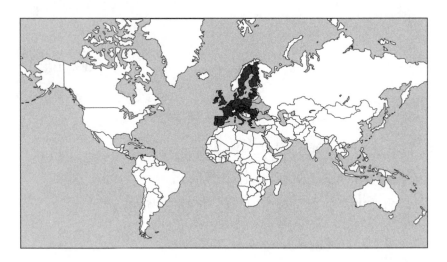

2. What service does an ISPA spokesman compare Internet service providers (ISPs) to, arguing against its responsibility to block online terrorist-related materials?

3. At the time of this article's publication in 2007, what responsibilities did British ISPs have?

P lacing instructions on how to make a bomb on the Internet will become a criminal offence across Europe under plans outlined by Brussels yesterday [July 3, 2007].

"It should simply not be possible to leave people free to instruct other people on the Internet on how to make a bomb—that has nothing to do with freedom of expression."

Arguments about freedom of expression will not be allowed to stand in the way of criminalising the publication of bomb-making information that could be used by terrorists, a senior EU [European Union] official said.

It will be part of a range of anti-terrorist proposals to be published in the autumn that will also include the collection of airline passenger data from every flight in and out of the

EU. The extension of measures was promised yesterday by Franco Frattini, the EU Justice Commissioner, after the British car bomb plot and the murder of Spanish tourists in Yemen.

Internet Service Providers Are Responsible

Internet service providers (ISPs) would face charges if they failed to block websites containing bomb-making instructions generated anywhere in the world, EU officials said.

"It should simply not be possible to leave people free to instruct other people on the Internet on how to make a bomb—that has nothing to do with freedom of expression," Mr Frattini said yesterday.

"My proposal will be to criminalise actions and instructions to make a bomb because it is too often that we discover websites that contain complete instructions for homemade bombs."

An Internet search yesterday instantly turned up a site that gave instructions on making a rudimentary bomb.

EU officials denied that it would be impossible to track down websites based in remote places, insisting that the local provider based in the EU could be held to account. One said: "You always need a provider here that gives you access to websites. They can decide technically which websites to allow. Otherwise how would China block Internet sites? There are no technological obstacles, only legal ones."

The Internet Service Providers' Association Disagrees

But the Internet Services Providers' Association (ISPA) said that it would fight any attempt to make ISPs criminally liable for content.

A spokesman described ISPs as "mere conduits", carriers of information, like the postal service. He added: "An ISP is not a publisher. It does not have editorial control over content posted on its servers by a third party."

How Do Terrorist Organizations Use the Internet?

The Internet is a powerful tool for terrorists, who use online message boards and chat rooms to share information, coordinate attacks, spread propaganda, raise funds, and recruit, experts say. According to Haifa University's Gabriel Weimann, whose research on the subject is widely cited, over the last ten years the number of terrorist sites has jumped from less than 100 to more than 4,800. "This has particularly taken off since the war in Iraq, as many of the insurgency groups there have many sites and message boards to help their network," says Michael Kern, a senior analyst at the SITE Institute, a Washington-based terrorist-tracking group.

Terrorist Web sites can serve as virtual training grounds, offering tutorials on building bombs, firing surface-to-air missiles, shooting at U.S. soldiers, and sneaking into Iraq from abroad. Terrorist sites also host messages and propaganda videos which help to raise morale and further the expansion of recruitment and fundraising networks.

Eben Kaplan, "Terrorists and the Internet,"
Council on Foreign Relations, May 12, 2006. www.cfr.org.

A [UK] government spokeswoman said that British-based sites that gave clear bomb making instructions could result in prosecution for encouragement to commit a terrorist act under the Terrorism Act 2006. But she added that there were problems of jurisdiction if the site was hosted outside Britain.

The EU can bring in basic criminal penalties in two ways—either with the unanimous approval of all 27 member states or in some policy areas where Britain has an opt-out. In either case, the basic proposal would then be put into effect by individual countries in their own legal systems.

The EU package will also include preparations for bioterrorism attacks and a European rapid-alert system for lost or stolen explosives. Mr Frattini added that a transatlantic passenger name record-sharing agreement between the EU and US completed last week should lead to the EU setting up its own system. This would require airlines to submit certain data such as passport and credit card details which could be used by national security agencies. The US can keep the data for 15 years but after the first seven it becomes "dormant" and can only be accessed case by case.

Tunisia Seeks to Control Citizens' Internet Use

Victoria Shannon

In the following viewpoint, Victoria Shannon reports from the 2005 United Nations summit meeting on communications issues in Tunisia, noting particularly that the vast increase in Internet use in Tunisia has resulted in the government's desire to control online content. According to Shannon, under President Zine Abidine ben Ali, hundreds of Web sites have been censored, Internet writers have been imprisoned, and the police force has been used to intimidate dissenters. Shannon explains that the Human Rights Watch organization is concerned about censorship and freedom of expression issues in Tunisia and throughout North Africa and the Middle East. Shannon is the technology editor for the International Herald Tribune, *an international English-language newspaper and online news source.*

As you read, consider the following questions:

1. According to Shannon, how many of Tunisia's 10 million residents were online in 2005, compared to a sparse 5,000 in 1998?

2. What other countries are mentioned by Human Rights Watch to have censorship and freedom of expression issues, according to Shannon?

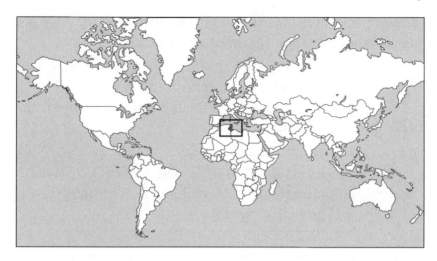

3. According to Eric Goldstein, Human Rights Watch's regional director, what kind of opportunity did the 2005 United Nations summit meeting present for Tunisia?

The hundreds of Tunisian flags waving across the capital city are like so many miniature red carpets unfurled in welcome for the 10,000 or so people, including scores of heads of state, who have come here to talk about the Internet this week [in November 2005].

Back in 1998, when Tunisia first proposed playing host to the United Nations summit meeting on communications issues, fewer than 5,000 of its residents were online. Today, Internet access in the North African nation has surged to nearly 790,000 out of a population of about 10 million.

The government says that nearly every public school is connected to the Web now, and it has subsidized about 400 low-cost Internet cafés nationwide.

Extreme Censorship

But Human Rights Watch, the New York-based public advocacy group, said in a report Tuesday that the government of President Zine Abidine ben Ali censors hundreds of Web sites, jails online writers for expressing their opinions, and uses police presence to harass and pressure opponents.

Ever since summit meeting officials started gathering here over the weekend, several journalists and representatives of public policy groups have complained of harassment, the breakup of civil meetings or worse.

The government [of Tunisia] censors hundreds of Web sites, jails online writers . . . , and uses police presence to harass and pressure opponents.

Like many developing nations, Tunisia's gains in spreading use of the Internet among its citizens are balanced by its desire to control that use, human rights observers say.

Many of the Web sites it has targeted as impolitic, for instance, are widely accessible on the free wireless connections the Tunisian government has provided inside Le Kram, the convention center near the airport where the World Summit on the Information Society officially begins on Wednesday. But at hotels outside the center, they are unreachable.

Le Monde, Libération and *Le Figaro* are some of the press Web sites that have been cut off in Tunisia, according to Eric Goldstein, Human Rights Watch's regional director. *Le Monde* recently criticized the Tunisian government for its treatment of the press in an editorial.

Basic Communications as a Human Right

In its report, called "False Freedom: Online Censorship in the Middle East and North Africa," Human Rights Watch also cited censorship and freedom of expression issues in Egypt and Iran, and said that the Syrian government "tampers with the very fabric of the Internet," restricting the use of basic communications tools that allow people to send e-mails and contact Web sites.

Human Rights Watch Reports on E-mail Surveillance in Tunisia

Tunisian activists uniformly told Human Rights Watch they believe the government monitors electronic communications. They told stories of e-mail arriving late or not at all, of responses to e-mails coming from third parties posing as the recipient when the intended recipient said he never received the original message, of e-mail inboxes being filled to saturation by repeated e-mails saying only, for example, "You are traitor." According to one account from a Web site of a human rights activist blocked in Tunisia, the Interior Ministry employs 500 "Internet police," most of whose time is spent reading e-mail. Sihem Bensedrine, the report's author, told Human Rights Watch that she had learned of the office's existence from a journalist who said he had seen the offices. Human Rights Watch was not able to confirm these allegations independently.

Human Rights Watch Publications,
"False Freedom: Online Censorship in the
Middle East and North Africa (Tunisia),"
November 2005. http://hrw.org.

Nouredine Kacem, a first secretary at Tunisia's UN mission in New York, played down the protests about his country's human rights record in an interview with the Associated Press. "Everywhere you go you have a protest. The people are not happy everywhere," Kacem said. "In Tunisia, we try to make the best of it. We are working very hard in human rights, the economy and so on. We are doing much better than other countries."

Goldstein argued that the summit meeting was an opportunity for the Tunisian government to show off its commitment to freedom of speech and human rights issues. But the incidents this week underscored the difficulty governments like Ben Ali's have in giving up control.

Periodical Bibliography

The following articles have been selected to supplement the diverse views presented in this chapter.

Peter Burrows — "Internet Censorship: A Community Effort; Saudi Arabia Relies on Its Citizens to Find Sites to Block," *Business Week*, November 24, 2008.

EFE World News Service — "Most-Banned Arab Web Page Is Edited in Spain," November 25, 2008.

Alastair Gee — "Russia's Dissident Bloggers Fear for Their Lives; The Gunshot Death of a Web Journalist Heightens Alarm About Efforts to Muzzle Dissent on the Internet," *U.S. News & World Report*, September 30, 2008.

The Independent (London) — "Wikipedia and the Art of Censorship," August 18, 2007.

Adam B. Kushner — "Repression 2.0," *Newsweek International*, April 14, 2008.

Joseph I. Lieberman, Leslie Harris, and John Morris — "Internet Accuracy: Should Online Sites Like YouTube Ban Postings by Groups the Government Identifies as Terrorists?" *CQ Researcher*, August 1, 2008.

Maclean's — "A Small Victory for Free Speech," October 27, 2008.

Jeffrey Rosen — "Free Speech on the Web: Is the Internet Really the Bastion of Free Expression That We Think It Is?" *New York Times Upfront*, January 12, 2009.

Tom Zeller Jr. — "The Internet Black Hole That Is North Korea," *New York Times*, October 23, 2006.

GLOBALVIEWPOINTS

CHAPTER 4

Political Expression

Political Message May Keep Song Out of Contest

Donald Macintyre

In the following viewpoint, Donald Macintyre reports on Euro-pean network Eurovision's threat to ban an Israeli band's song entry from its annual contest due to its outspoken political mes-sage. According to Macintyre, the controversial song "Push the Button," by the band Teapacks, has been deemed by some critics as "inappropriate" for the contest, because it criticizes Israel's own politics and security threats while acknowledging the foreign militant attacks. Macintyre, an award-winning journalist, has been The Independent's *Jerusalem correspondent since 2004. His career at* The Independent *started with his position as po-litical editor, and he served as chief political commentator for eight years.*

As you read, consider the following questions:

1. According to Macintyre, how has "Push the Button" been interpreted?
2. How does lead singer and song writer Kobi Oz describe the song?
3. How does Yoav Ginai of the Israel Broadcasting Author-ity describe Kobi Oz?

Eurovision [the world's largest international broadcast server controlled by the European Broadcasting Union] is threatening to ban Israel's entry for its annual song contest because of its "inappropriate" political message. "Push the Button", the song from one of Israel's most experienced and popular bands, Teapacks, has lyrics that go to the heart of the country's most prevalent security fears, but in tones tinged with irony.

Controversial Political Message

The words of the song—in English, French and Hebrew,—have already been interpreted as addressing fears of a strike by Iran as well as attacks by Palestinian militants. In one verse the band sing: "The world is full of terror/ If someone makes an error/ He's gonna blow us up to biddy biddy kingdom come/ There are some crazy rulers they hide and try to fool us/ With demonic, technologic willingness to harm."

Kjell Ekholm, an organiser of the contest, said: "It's absolutely clear that this kind of message is not appropriate for the competition." But the threat may say as much about Eurovision's dogged preference for the bland at all costs as about the song itself.

"We are not working to make nice to everyone. Real art provokes responses and provokes people into arguing."

The band's lead singer Kobi Oz, who is of Tunisian extraction, and is known for his witty and enigmatic lyrics, comes from Sderot [a city in Western Negev, in the South District of Israel], which has born the brunt of Qassam rockets from Gaza, and as a member of a Jewish family from an Arab country is a leading exponent of "Mizrahi cool".

Another verse says: "Messages are exploding on me/ Rockets are flying and landing on me." But the song also takes a

Kobi Oz, the Lead Singer of Teapacks, Responds to a Controversial Lyric in His Song

"The song has a line that talks about 'some crazy leaders,' but we didn't mention names. The state of Israel has gone through enough so that it can laugh at terrorism. The Israelis chose the song because that is the best way: not to be afraid, but to laugh in their faces."

Steven Erlanger,
"Eurovision Contest Weighs Ban on Israeli Band's Entry,"
International Herald Tribune, *March 2, 2007. www.iht.com.*

swipe at the country's own politics as well as security threats, saying Israelis are caught between "political tricks and kidnapping".

Not a Typical Song Entry

The song also deliberately projects itself as a counterpoint to the anodyne lyrics of previous Eurovision entries, from Israel as well as other countries. In one section, the band sing: "Here we are in the pre-finals with a song that isn't about salaam [Arabic for peace], red is not just a colour, it's more like blood."

Oz said that the song, an occasionally Queen-like musical blend of rap, rock and more oriental sound, was "multicultural", adding for good measure: "We are not working to make nice to everyone. Real art provokes responses and provokes people into arguing." At one point the band sing, in what could be construed as a reference to Israel's own nuclear arsenal: "If it continues to be frightening, then only then I will say I'm gonna push the button, push the button, push the button, push the button."

Yoav Ginai, the head of the Israel Broadcasting Authority's judging committee, has described Oz as "one of the most unique and original composers in the country".

Mr Ginai speaks with authority as the man who write the lyrics for the song "Diva", which won the Eurovision Song Contest in 1998 in Birmingham for Israel. The song also generated headlines across the world because it was sung by Dana, a transsexual.

Wha, Wha the police

Weeoo, weeoo a rescue team

Here it is in the semi-finals without salaam

Red is not only a colour, it's more like blood.

Islamic Governments Collide with Freedom of Expression

Maryam Namazie

Maryam Namazie, in a speech given at the 2008 World Humanist Congress in Washington, D.C., addresses her views on freedom of expression under Islamic governments. Namazie emphasizes the importance of not only criticizing and challenging religion, but doing so in combination with the issue of political power. Using the political Islamic movement as her focus, Namazie argues that in order for Islamic countries to progress, Islam must be eradicated from the "public sphere." To do so, she claims, freedom of expression, particularly the freedom to criticize religion and politics, is essential. Namazie is a human rights activist, commentator, and broadcaster who focuses on issues in Iran and the Middle East. Such issues include women's rights, cultural relativism, secularism, humanism, religion, Islam, and political Islam.

As you read, consider the following questions:

1. When, according to Namazie, does freedom of expression matter most?
2. According to Namazie, describing beliefs with what adjective suppresses freedom of expression?
3. What action does Namazie call a "historical duty and task"?

Maryam Namazie, "Freedom of Expression and Political Islam," *Scoop*, June 24, 2008. www.scoop.co.nz. Reproduced by permission of the author.

Freedom of expression matters. It is not a luxury, a western value and it's certainly not up for sale (though obviously governments and the UN [United Nations] mistakenly think it to be so).

Sometimes—actually more often than not—it is all we have.

But like many other rights and freedoms, it becomes most significant and finds real meaning when it comes to criticising that which is taboo, forbidden, sacred.

I think [criticism of religion] has always been an important vehicle for progress and the betterment of humanity's lot in centuries past.

Freedom of expression matters most, therefore, when it comes to criticising religion.

I think this criticism has always been an important vehicle for progress and the betterment of humanity's lot in centuries past. This is also true today in the 21st century and particularly with regard to Islam.

Of course Islam is no different from other religions. You can find just as much misogyny, cruelty and inhumanity in the Bible or other religious books as you can in the Koran. And I don't think Islam, Christianity, Judaism or what have you are fundamentally any different from Scientology or Moon's Unification Church, which are deemed to be cults endangering social and personal development. After all, isn't that what religion is?

But even so, today—as we speak—there is still a distinction to be made between religion in general and Islam in particular but for no other reason than that it is the ideology behind a movement that is, in many places, part and parcel of the state, the law, criminal so-called 'justice' or injustice system or sharia law and educational system.

I think this point is key for a principled criticism of Islam and more importantly a progressive and humane response to the outrage of our era.

A Duty to Criticise

This means, firstly, that we have a duty to criticise Islam; this goes beyond the mere right to and freedom of speech and expression.

I am always taken aback by complaints about how reports on Islam often concentrate on the subject of violence and rarely focus on the reality of Islam in everyday life. In fact, though, the reality of Islam in everyday life is far more violent than anything that can be fathomed. Entire generations slaughtered over decades—long before 9/11 [2001]—and buried in mass graves in Iran, Iraq, Afghanistan and elsewhere.

The human cost of Islam in power is enough of a reason—the only necessary reason—to make criticism a task and duty.

After all, it is impossible—let me repeat, impossible—to challenge a political movement that has wreaked havoc primarily for the people of the Middle East and North Africa if you are not allowed to fully and unequivocally criticise its ideology and banner.

I know some say that the problem is not Islam but the fundamentalist interpretation of Islam. But in my opinion, you can't have Islamic feminism, Islamic reformism, Islamic democracy, Islamic human rights, and moderate interpretations of Islam when it is in power.

Of course there are innumerable Muslims or those labelled as such who have humanist, secularist, moderate, egalitarian, atheist, Communist and other progressive viewpoints but this is not one and the same with Islam in power being as such.

In my opinion, a 'moderate' or 'reformed' religion is one that has been pushed back and reigned in by an enlightenment. And not before.

A Survey of the Role of Islam in Political Life, 2004

Based on Muslims	Currently plays a large role		Should play a large role	
	Men	Women	Men	Women
Indonesia	87	86	84	82
Nigeria	80	85	66	79
Lebanon	65	65	64	62
Senegal	65	64	46	42
Mali	63	60	73	66
Jordan	58	48	85	66
Bangladesh	53	51	83	85
Pakistan	52	64	91	85
Uzbekistan	48	60	43	46
Turkey	45	45	40	44
Tanzania	16	13	15	22

Question asked of Muslim respondents only.
Question not permitted in Egypt.

TAKEN FROM: Nicole Speulda and Mary McIntosh, "Global Gender Gaps," The Pew Research Center for the People and the Press, May 13, 2004. http://people-press.org.

Removing Religion from the Public Sphere

But criticism of Islam alone is not enough if it does not also come with a criticism of the political Islamic movement and religion industry. The right wing's criticism of Islam and its sudden championing of women's rights in the Middle East—whilst legislating religious morality and misogyny here at home—self-servingly ignores the main issue at hand, which is religion and political power.

If we are going to win this battle again—as in centuries past—we have to push Islam and religion out of the public sphere. Full stop.

And for this, freedom of expression and freedom to criticise religion are key.

I don't think we can compromise on this because too many lives are at stake. And in my opinion compromise includes the misguided liberal attempts at building interfaith coalitions or deeming all religions and beliefs as equally valid. It also includes the more reactionary sorts of appeasement such as that of the recently launched Tony Blair Faith Foundation, which aims 'to promote respect and understanding about the world's major religions and show how faith is a powerful force for good in the modern world.'

Religion wouldn't need one public relations campaign after another if it was so good, now would it?

Religion wouldn't need one public relations campaign after another if it was so good, now would it? Even calling it 'faith' and avoiding the term religion won't get around the fact that it is the genocidaire of our age.

Either way—misguided or purely out of economic and political interests—these endeavours only serve to increase, justify and consolidate the role of religion in society—and are part of the problem rather than any solution.

In my opinion, you have to choose.

You must either defend the human being or you must defend Islam and religion. You can't defend both because they are incompatible with and antithetical to each other.

Criticism of Religion Should Not Be Equated with Personal Attacks

Of course this doesn't mean that people don't have a right to religion or atheism. Of course they do but as a private affair. Having the right to a religion or belief does not include the right not to be offended or the right to have your belief or religion respected, tolerated, and deemed equal and equally valid. Concepts such as rights, equality, and respect raised vis-à-vis individuals are nowadays more and more applicable to religion at the expense of people and their rights and freedoms. And that's why a criticism of religion is deemed racism, defamatory, libellous—again concepts originally raised regarding people, not religion and beliefs!

Islamists and their apologists have succeeded in blurring the distinction between individuals and beliefs. Their use of rights and anti-racist language—at least in the West—are devious ways of silencing criticism and opposition.

Of course the human being is sacred and worthy of the highest respect, rights and equality but not religions, beliefs, cultures.

Having the right to a religion or belief does not include the right not to be offended.

Clearly, criticism of Islam and Mohammad are not racist or an attack on Muslims any more than Christ in a nappy in 'Jerry Springer: The Opera' is an attack or racism against Christians. Actually it is racist to see Islam and Muslims as one and the same and Islamists and Muslims as one and the same. It is racist to imply that this is the belief of all those deemed to be Muslim when in fact it is the belief system of a ruling class and its parasitical imams, organisations and states. It is racist to imply that people choose to live the way they are forced to. That they actually deserve no better and that their rights are culturally relative. Not that they do but even if everyone believed that women were subhuman and gays perverts, criticism of a belief is not one and the same as attacking the person who holds the belief. Female genital mutilation [FGM] is a good example. You can criticise and condemn the belief in and practice of FGM, but this does not amount to an attack on women and girls who are mutilated or who support the practice.

This type of politics—knowingly or unwittingly—attempts to make criticism of Islam and religion more difficult. Defining certain beliefs as sacred is a tool for the suppression of society. Saying expression offends is an attempt to restrict it.

I still find it astonishing how religion in power hangs the likes of sweet 16 Atefeh Rajabi [Iranian girl sentenced to death by an Iranian judge for allegedly committing "acts in compatible with chastity"] and stones Maryam Ayoubi [persecuted for having sex outside of marriage by the Islamic regime in Iran] to death—even specifying by law the size of the stone to be used—in Iran or sentences Parwiz Kambakhsh to death in Afghanistan for downloading materials critical of women and Islam from the Internet and it is criticism of Islam that is offensive!

The Defense of Secularism and the Criticism of Militarism Are Essential

In the face of this onslaught, a defence of freedom of expression and a criticism of religion, Islam and political Islam is an historical duty and task but it has to be based within a politics that puts people first, that holds the human being—and nothing else—sacred, if it is to have real meaning and affect real change.

It has to be done in conjunction with a defence of secularism—as the strict separation of religion from the state—rather than mere neutrality. It has to be done alongside a defence of universal rights, citizenship rights, and a humanity without labels other than human.

And it has to be done alongside a criticism of US led militarism—particularly important to say as we are here in Washington, DC. This is not a clash between western and Islamic values. Progressive values were fought for and gained by the working class and progressive social movements and so belong to all of humanity. If we don't look at it in this way we will make friends with false allies and also fail to make links and show real solidarity with a vast majority fighting on the frontlines against Islam in power and US led militarism in places like Iran.

Also, this is not a clash of civilisations but actually the clash of the uncivilised. Human civilisation exists despite political Islam and US-led militarism and is very much at odds with it. After all, political Islam was brought to centre stage during the Cold War as a green belt around the then Soviet Union and as a response to the rise of the left and working class movement in the Iranian revolution.

Western governments have never had a problem with Islam in power—their only problem was that it had moved out of its sphere of influence since 9/11. In fact, their 'interventions' in Iraq for example has only strengthened this movement. In the New World Order, in fact, US-led militarism needs and feeds off political Islam. They are two sides of one coin, with the same capacity for infinite violence and brutality, the same reliance on religion and the same bleak message for the people of the world.

Freedom of expression is one of the only means we have at our disposal to resist both camps of reaction and to protect humanity.

We have to defend it unequivocally and unconditionally.

Americans Learn That Online Political Expression Can Have Repercussions in the Workplace

Rebecca Knowles and Lillian Cunningham

In the following viewpoint, Rebecca Knowles and Lillian Cunningham address the increasing use of the Internet as a political platform for American youth. Knowles and Cunningham acknowledge a common misconception among young Americans—the belief that because political expression is protected under the First Amendment, outspoken political opinions cannot affect one's position at the workplace. Many sources cited by the authors reveal that job candidates are being discarded and established employees fired because of their political views found online. Knowles and Cunningham are youth and politics reporters for Medill, a news service based at Northwestern University's School of Journalism.

As you read, consider the following questions:

1. According to Knowles and Cunningham, how many states do not protect employees from being fired due to their political opinions?

2. What information did the ExecuNet surveys of 15,000 job recruiters and executives provide, according to the authors?

3. What is one instance cited in this article of an employee being fired because of an expression of political opinion?

Facebook face-offs. MySpace mudslinging. As the newbies in [2008's] presidential throw-down, throngs of young people are finding their political voice and, of course, they're finding it often with little restraint online. But that free speech could come at a cost.

With political expression traveling at warp speed online, bosses can instantly find that diatribe posted about [Barack] Obama or [John] McCain and they can wield the ax for it just as quickly. The labor codes in 48 states have never protected employees from being fired for their political views. But, then again, personal information has never been so readily available.

A Common Misconception

"I think young people going in are under the assumption they are free to engage in free speech so long as it doesn't take you away from your work," said Jason Mattera, a 24-year-old spokesman for Young America's Foundation, a national conservative organization focused on college campuses.

That assumption has translated into a willingness among young people to take their politics to the Web. "People are getting really involved online," said Sean Sullivan, an 18-year-old student at Grove City College, Pa. "It's become really popular with the campaigns this year."

Bruce Barry, who wrote the book *Speechless: The Erosion of Free Expression in the American Workplace*, said, "We all have this magical view of free speech." Young people's lack of work experience contributes to their misconception that they can say whatever they want about politics without workplace repercussions, he said.

The result is an election-year Internet riddled with vicious opinion blogs, partisan Facebook groups and a near free-for-all when it comes to young people's political expression.

Young people [have a] misconception that they can say whatever they want about politics without workplace repercussions.

"In a year like this, there are fewer and fewer of us left who don't have strong opinions," said Stephen Rothberg, president and founder of CollegeRecruiter.com, an online recruitment and career advising site for young adults. "But once you post that information online, it's never really gone. And I think it comes as a shock to most (job) applicants just how much employers are digging into their digital dirt."

Lauren Koehler, 20, a senior at Boston University, said, "For a long time, I think people felt like the Internet was a massive safe harbor. You could say things online that you couldn't in real life because it wouldn't come back to you. But as we've gone on, more and more people have had their 'real' lives affected by the things they post."

Internet Background Checks

Professional networking organization ExecuNet e-mailed surveys to 15,000 recruiters and executives last year to determine their use of online resources in background checks. The vast majority of those who responded said they use online search engines and networking sites to learn more about candidates. Nearly half acknowledged they disqualified some job seekers because of information found online, ranging from evidence of drug use to extreme political views.

"It's that kind of stuff that bothers me," Koehler said. "That I may miss out on opportunities because of something I posted on the Internet."

Online searches are becoming an increasingly routine part of the hiring process, said Brad Karsh, former director of talent acquisition at Leo Burnett advertising in Chicago.

"My advice is to shy away from political things on your resume because they do alienate certain people, and I tell candidates not to put anything online they wouldn't put on their resume," said Karsh, who now runs a career consultancy called JobBound.

"I'm not going to look at, say, all 500 people whose resumes I receive," said Karsh. "But if I narrow my list down to 10 or even to the final two, I might just go online and see what I can find."

"Stay away from attack content, viciously attacking candidates," said CollegeRecruiter's Rothberg. "If you write, 'I don't like Hillary because she's a woman,' you'll have a major problem with any employer."

Adult Employees Fired for Political Views

While the Labor Department doesn't keep statistics on the reasons for hirings and firings, there have been a few high-profile incidents in which employers dismissed workers for their political views. And some of those targeted were adults.

During the 2004 presidential race, Lynne Gobbell of Moulton, Ala., now 45, lost her job at Enviromate, a housing-insulation maker, for pasting a Kerry/Edwards bumper sticker on her car. Phil Geddes, the company owner and staunch supporter of President Bush, suggested Gobbell could either "work for him or work for John Kerry."

By a lucky happenstance for Gobbell, getting canned from her old job turned into an opportunity. When Kerry's cam-

Social Networking Website Data Reveals the Popularity of Online American Politics

Democratic candidates	myspace.com Friends	You Tube™ Channel views
Barack Obama	169,397	11,098,217
Hillary Clinton	133,684	849,842
John Edwards	47,936	616,160
Dennis Kucinich	30,141	481,271
Bill Richardson	20,910	534,450
Joe Biden	14,300	286,112
Mike Gravel	9,353	632,377
Christopher Dodd	8,890	414,548
Republican candidates		
Ron Paul	56,769	3,323,091
John McCain	40,948	464,081
Mitt Romney	30,992	738,988
Sam Brownback	11,313	484,469
Rudy Giuliani	7,434	621,155
Duncan Hunter	6,908	360,353
Mike Huckabee	6,053	184,781
Tom Tancredo	3,989	424,132

TAKEN FROM: Derek Pokora, "The Influence of Web 2.0 on American Politics," Wikinomics, August 24, 2007. http://www.wikinomics.com.

paign heard what happened to her, he called Gobbell personally to offer her a job with his campaign, and she jumped at the chance.

The same year, then 35-year-old graphic designer Glen Hiller of Berkeley Springs, W.Va., was fired by Octavo Designs in Frederick, Md., after shouting comments criticizing the Iraq war during a rally for Bush. Octavo said Hiller embarrassed the company and the client who had provided the tickets to the rally.

And that political expression was tame compared with some of the out-there opinions young people are putting online this time around.

Young Adults Have Reasons to Be Cautious

Just sift through Facebook, a social networking site that allows its (predominantly young) users to create personal profiles and join online groups. It's hard not to stumble across political groups with inflammatory slogans, such as, "Life's a bitch, why vote for one? Anti-Hillary '08," a group with more than 15,000 members.

Others include "George Bush is a Fascist" and "I think therefore I am not Republican." That's only the beginning, and the language of many others is too offensive to print.

Some young adults are exercising more caution online, especially with the unemployment rate sitting at 4.9 percent.

Some [young adults are] using the Internet as a clean slate for job applications instead of a soapbox for political opinions.

"We're seeing a significant uptick in nervousness by students," Rothberg said. "They're pessimistic about getting multiple job offers after graduation."

This pessimism could be trickling down to young adults' online behaviors. Some are making a point of keeping politics off-line, using the Internet as a clean slate for job applications instead of a soapbox for political opinions.

For Liz Egan, 23, an intern at the Heritage Foundation, a conservative think tank in Washington, her passion for politics doesn't make it to the Web. "There are a lot of employers who are shameless about getting their employees to find people on

Facebook for them," Egan said. "I'm not rushing out to have a political blog because that's just not how I want to be defined."

Egan's not the only young adult weighing the value of going viral with political musings against future career prospects. "Students, especially seniors in college, are so nervous and cautious about jobs," said Margot Locker, 22, a senior at Northwestern University. "I can see how people my age would be reluctant to put anything controversial including their political views online."

Politically Outspoken

For Locker, who has worked on Sen. Hillary Clinton's campaign and who started the Facebook group "Northwestern for Hillary," being politically active is more important than keeping quiet to protect job prospects.

"There's some personal information I'll be cautious about, but politically, I'll put all my views online," she said. "It's not even a second thought for me."

She's not alone. "No, I definitely didn't take the spineless route," said Mattera of Young America's Foundation. "It takes guts to say, 'This is what I believe in and I'm going to deal with the consequences.' If anyone denies me work in the future because I'm a conservative, so be it; everyone should wear their beliefs like a badge of honor."

Some free-speech advocates, such as *Speechless* author Barry, worry that as college advisers and hiring managers urge careful management of online profiles, fewer young people are likely to risk going public with their political views.

"University placement offices tell the kids, 'Think about what you're doing,' and the political identity is an interesting variation," said Barry, who teaches management and sociology at Vanderbilt University.

CollegeRecruiter's Rothberg is equally apprehensive. "I hope we don't turn into a society that's afraid to be politically engaged because it might harm a job application 20 years down the road," Rothberg said. "But it's going to happen."

Tibet's Freedom of Expression Is Questioned After the Arrest of a Political Demonstrator

Phurbu Thinley

In the following viewpoint, Phurbu Thinley reports on the arrest of Ronggay A'drak, a Tibetan nomad from Lithang, for his political demonstration during a government function. At that function, A'drak declared his desire for Tibet's independence, called for the return of the Dalai Lama, and asked fellow Tibetans to stop fighting amongst themselves. According to Thinley, many who were present agreed with A'drak's opinions, leading to a mass demonstration from the audience. Thinley reports that after A'drak's arrest, many locals demanded his release, holding their own political demonstration in defense of Tibetans' right to freedom of opinion and expression. Thinley is a writer and photographer for Phayul.com, an English-language Tibetan news Web site.

As you read, consider the following questions:

1. What slogans did A'drak say during his political demonstration, as cited by Thinley?

2. According to the Tibetan Centre for Human Rights and Democracy, what did local villagers say they would do in the name of freedom of expression if A'drak was not released by a certain time?

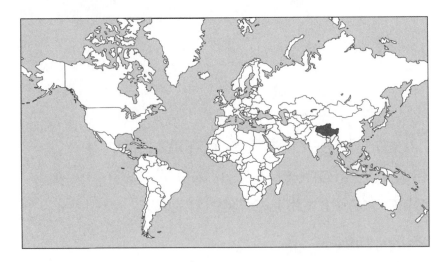

3. What is the mission of the Tibetan Centre for Human Rights and Democracy, according to Thinley?

A Tibetan nomad from Lithang was arrested in Tibet yesterday [August 1, 2007] for staging a political demonstration during an official function, according to Tibetan Centre for Human Rights and Democracy (TCHRD).

According to confirmed information received by TCHRD, Ronggay A'drak, a Tibetan nomad from Lithang, was arrested for staging a political demonstration during the official function for the 80th Founding Anniversary of the People's Liberation Army (PLA) organised by the Lithang County Government on Wednesday (August 1, 2007).

A large number of people from Lithang area were reported to have come to witness the official function and the famous annual horse race festival popular in the area.

A Peaceful Political Demonstration

Just before the start of the official function at around 11:00am, when the Chief guest, other officials and the general public were present, Ronggay A'drak, a 52-year-old Tibetan nomad from Youru Village, Lithang County, Kardze Tibetan Autonomous Prefecture (TAP), went up to the stage to offer a traditional Tibetan scarf to Lithang Kyabgyon—the Chief Lama of Lithang Monastery. Ronggay A'drak then seized the microphone and, before a large gathering, shouted slogans like: "The Dalai Lama should return to Tibet", "Release Panchen Lama", "Tibet wants Independence".

He then insisted on Tibetan people to stop fighting among themselves on the land, water dispute and on the collection of *Yartsa Gunbu*, a caterpillar fungus.

Last month, the Associated Press reported that a gun battle between Tibetan groups feuding over access to the lucrative wild caterpillar fungus left up to six people dead and more than 110 injured in a Tibetan area of Sichuan Province. The fighting is said to have broken out after County officials made no move to intervene, despite knowledge of the conflicting tension in the area over the land demarcation.

Later, Ronggay A'drak climbed down from the stage and in the presence of the Officials and whole crowd, went straight to Naglu Tenzin, a monk who is said to be actively involved in the Chinese "Patriotic education campaign" and told him to denounce his double standard in dealing with the religious affairs of the monastery.

A'drak then climbed back to the stage and continued shouting slogans, which made the general public to join him in unison. He was finally arrested by Kardze local police and was taken away to an unknown place.

Villagers Demonstrate for Nomad's Release in the Name of Freedom of Expression

According to TCHRD's press statement, sensing fear for the safety of Ronggay A'drak, scores of people from Lithang Yonru Village went to Lithang County Office to demand his immediate release and to ascertain his whereabouts and condition. They even demonstrated inside the compound of the County

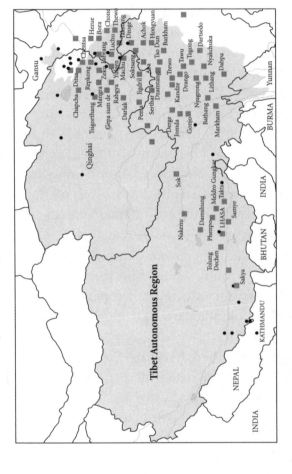

Sites of Tibetan Demonstrations and Protests, 2008

Sites compiled from various sources where protests are reported to have taken place between March 10, and April 5, 2008.

TAKEN FROM: "Sites of Tibetan Demonstrations and Protests," International Campaign for Tibet, April 5, 2008. http://www.savetibet.org.

office calling for his immediate release and respect of Tibetan people's right to freedom of expression and opinion.

According to the centre's statement, quoting reliable sources, a few people even broke into the County Office to demand his immediate release. Sensing further escalation of tension, the police officer even threatened the villagers by firing a pistol into the air.

The Tibetan people, unmoved by the threats, weathered incessant rain on that day to proceed forward with their demand. It was learnt that the villagers finally returned to their place only after the officials agreed to release Ronggay A'drak the next day at 2:00pm.

Quoting another source, TCHRD's press release states, "While returning to their place, the villagers called for Tibetans, followers of the Dalai Lama and pro-independence to join them. And they even told that if the authorities did not release Ronggay A'drak today by 2:00pm they will organize a mass demonstration in front of the detention centre 'no matter how much restriction officials put on them.'"

The situation in Lithang County is known to be very tense. Strangely, this time the local officials' compliance with the demands of local Tibetans was unprecedented. However, it is difficult to predict the future course of the case.

"Freedom of expression is a fundamental human right which is a prerequisite to the enjoyment of all human rights."

The Tibetan Centre for Human Rights

TCHRD has expressed its deepest concern at the arrest of Ronggay A'drak for exercising his political rights and has demanded his immediate release.

"The People's Republic of China (PRC) should abide by the rights guaranteed in the constitution and other major international covenants and treaties which she is party to," TCHRD's press release urges.

Stating, "Freedom of expression is a fundamental human right which is a prerequisite to the enjoyment of all human rights," in its statement, TCHRD has called upon the support of human rights groups and the international community in securing A'drak's release.

The Centre deems the case as an outright clampdown on the freedom of opinion and expression and says that it will continue to monitor the situation and would update on the issue as and when further information surfaces.

The Tibetan Centre for Human Rights and Democracy (TCHRD) is the first Tibetan non-governmental organization (NGO) to be formed with the mission "to highlight the human rights situation in Tibet and to promote principles of democracy in the Tibetan community." TCHRD is independent of the Tibetan Government-in-Exile, and is based in Dharamsala, India.

Northern Ireland's Political Murals Are Censored for the Peace Process

Brendan O'Neill

In the following viewpoint, Brendan O'Neill describes the efforts of Protestant East Belfast and Catholic West Belfast to "decommission paramilitary murals" in the capital of Northern Ireland. According to O'Neill, old political murals with violent themes will be replaced by murals that depict more neutral subjects that highlight the cultures of Protestants and Catholics in Ireland. O'Neill points out that while this project aims to contribute to the peace process, some artists, curators, and commissioners among others feel that rules dictating what can and cannot be displayed on public spaces are evidence of censorship. O'Neill is a journalist and the editor of Spiked Online, *a London-based Internet magazine observing issues of culture, society, and politics. O'Neill has written articles for such publications as* The Guardian *and* The Christian Science Monitor.

As you read, consider the following questions:

1. How many political murals as of 2005, did Methodist minister Gary Mason persuade leaders of the Protestant paramilitary to have repainted with more positive cultural images?

Brendan O'Neill, "Belfast Murals Reflect a Change of Art," *The Christian Science Monitor*, December 14, 2005. Reproduced by permission of the author.

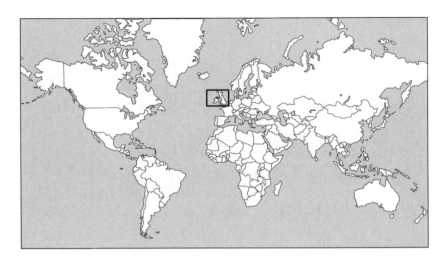

2. According to Deirdre Mackel, in what way is the mur24 project censored?

3. What does gallery director Pauline Hadaway claim the repainting of the murals obscures?

On a pale wintry morning in working-class East Belfast, hooded men with guns seem to follow me. These ghosts from a long-gone conflict lurk on the walls, peering through the slits of their balaclavas at kids skipping to school and a woman lugging home her weekly shop.

Protestant terrorists, who fought to defend the Union between Northern Ireland and Britain during the Troubles [a period of conflict between Irish republican and loyalist paramilitary organizations from the late 1960s until the late 1990s peace process], may be mostly inactive now (give or take the occasional internal feud). But here, they still stare down from hand-painted murals at the gable ends of terraced housing, their masked mugs a permanent, if patchy and fading reminder of yesteryear's war.

Methodist Minister Urges the Decommission of Political Murals

In all of Northern Ireland there are hundreds of these sectarian murals, done by artists from both sides of the conflict. The Rev. Gary Mason, a cheery Methodist minister, wants to exorcise this ghostly presence from East Belfast. He heads a project to "decommission paramilitary murals" and replace them with more positive celebrations of Protestant culture.

"Imagine a wee boy or girl looking out of their bedroom window and seeing burly guys with rifles. What does that do to them, psychologically?" he asks. "It doesn't only say violence is acceptable, which would be bad enough; it says violence is something to be celebrated in colorful paintings."

"We've taken the gun out of politics; now we need to take it out of the murals."

In often tortuous talks that began in 2002 and continue now, Mr. Mason has coaxed leaders of Protestant paramilitary groups to give up nine murals which have been painted over with images of "cultural treasures we can be proud of," he says. One of the "post-para" murals shows George Best, the East Belfast boy who revolutionized soccer in the 1960s and died recently; another shows C.S. Lewis, also born in East Belfast, alongside scenes from his most famous book—now a big box office flick—*The Lion, the Witch and the Wardrobe.*

"Now there's peace, why should we have war on our walls?" asks Mason. "We've taken the gun out of politics; now we need to take it out of the murals."

Transition from Political to Peaceful

Over the past 20 years, Belfast has become famous (perhaps infamous) for its paramilitary murals, visual depictions of its "troubled" times. In Catholic republican areas, street paintings celebrated the Irish Republican Army [IRA]; in Protestant loyalist areas they paid tribute to a host of splintered violent outfits such as the UDA (Ulster Defense Association), the UVF (Ulsters Volunteer Force), the UFF (Ulster Freedom Fighters). Things are starting to change. With the help of generous city government funding, community activists are replacing these symbols of war with advertisements for peace.

"The new murals can contribute to the peace process," says Bill Rolston, a sociologist at the University of Ulster, who for 20 years has photographed and analyzed this street art-cum-propaganda (not for nothing is he known as "Mr. Murals").

I meet him at the Europa Hotel in the city center, itself a glass and concrete testament to how much has changed here. It once had the unenviable title of "the most bombed hotel in Europe," targeted 11 times by the Irish Republican Army.

"The old murals captured the two communities' aspirations and anxieties," he says. "The new murals, coming through slowly and tentatively, suggest that people are keen to look forward, not back."

The new murals, often funded by local government, come with conditions attached. There are strict rules about what can be depicted—and this has some artists and curators asking: "Well, is it really community art?"

"Peace Murals" Are Censored

After spending the morning with George Best and C.S. Lewis in Protestant East Belfast, I take a cab to Catholic West Belfast.

We drive through the Falls Road, the heart of republican Belfast—past the Sinn Fein offices, a mural paying tribute to the IRA hunger strikers who starved themselves to death in 1981, and graffiti saying "Victory to the ClRA" (the Continuity Irish Republican Army).

An Argument Against Decommissioning the Original Belfast Murals

Brought up as a republican in West Belfast, I have no sympathy with loyalist murals that glorified attacks on my community. In fact, my sentiment is reserved for memories of my friends and I audaciously (or perhaps recklessly) trying to deface these murals in the early hours of damp Belfast mornings. And yet, I have serious issues with officialdom's attempts to replace the authentic voice of Belfast's working-class communities with state-sponsored art. . . .

Offensive or not, loyalist murals were the authentic and spontaneous artistic expressions of local communities. There is nothing spontaneous or authentic about the new murals, which are being pushed by the British government and local councils. Despite the language of 'inclusion' that now dominates all political discourse in Northern Ireland, it is clear that the old murals are excluded in the re-imaging process and only images acceptable to the authorities will be included.

Kevin Rooney,
"Northern Ireland: Painting over the Cracks,"
Spiked Online, *September 9, 2008. www.spiked-online.com.*

At the offices of the Upper Springfield Development Trust, Deirdre Mackel explains the thinking behind the new "peace murals."

"Our aim is to get the local community, especially young people, involved in painting them," she says. "It gives them a sense of ownership of their surroundings."

She has commissioned some quite stunning work, including the Whiterock Children's Centre Mural, a celebration of Celtic myths painted by a professional artist with the help of local kids; and *Tá ár gCultúr beo* (Gaelic for, "Our Culture is Alive"), a sprawling 60-foot mural that celebrates the Irish landscape.

But certain things are off limits. "We are censored, yes," says Ms. Mackel, whose trust is funded in part by the Northern Ireland government. "We cannot paint any flags or emblems, and we have to steer clear of politics." That's one reason many of the new murals in this part of Belfast depict mythical events—red-haired beauties on white horses that are unlikely to offend anybody.

Pauline Hadaway, director of the Belfast Exposed photography gallery, which recently published a book on the changing face of murals, worries that making local communities look nice is "a smoke screen obscuring our failure to address important social and economic questions" in East and West Belfast, which are among the poorest communities in the United Kingdom.

The Impact of Change

Back in East Belfast, the George Best mural has become an impromptu shrine to his memory, with locals leaving flowers and notes of condolence. And this, says Gary Mason, proves that the new murals are about more than "tinkering with the way things look."

"They can make a real difference to how people feel. And companies will be more willing to invest in our communities if there aren't pictures of gunmen everywhere," he says. "This kind of art can help to make a better future."

Periodical Bibliography

The following articles have been selected to supplement the diverse views presented in this chapter.

Africa News Service   "Critical Journalists Could Be Viewed as 'Supporting Terrorists' and Arrested, Warns Attorney General," November 19, 2008.

Africa News Service   "A Journalist Jailed for Eight Months for 'Damaging Former Minister's Reputation,'" October 5, 2007.

Jamshid Ahmadi   "In Defence of Human Rights in Iran," *Iran Times International*, December 26, 2008.

Matthew Clark and   "Why Women Now Lead the Dissident Fight in Sara Miller Llana   Cuba," *The Christian Science Monitor*, July 24, 2008.

Melissa Hancock   "Egypt Faces Barriers to Democracy: Cairo Continues to Stifle Freedom of Expression, Political Opposition and Is Accused of Rolling Back Steps Towards Democracy, While Seeking to Reassert Itself on the Regional Diplomatic Stage," *Middle East Economic Digest*, November 7, 2008.

Richard Seymour   "Middle East Bloggers Set Cat Among the Pigeons. (Imprisonment of Abdel Kareem Nabil Soliman)," *The Middle East*, April 2008.

The Toronto Star   "Montreal in Bid to Unmask Protesters; Activists Say Ban a Blow to Freedom of Speech, but Police Say It Would Deter Violent Protests," January 25, 2009.

U.S. News & World Report   "Jailed Chinese Dissident Hu Jia Is Honored; Beijing Denounces the Action and Threatens Europe with Reprisals," October 23, 2008.

For Further Discussion

Chapter 1: Freedom of the Press

1. Self-censorship is discussed in the viewpoint of Kirstin Hausen. Using examples from this chapter, explain how governments can provoke self-censorship among publishers, journalists, and other writers.

2. Slovakia's culture minister says of Slovakia's media law, "It does not jeopardise freedom of the press. It merely upgrades the interest of the public above the interest of the publishers." Using examples from this chapter, take the position of a press-controlling government, or of an editor or writer, and explain your case as to why or why not government's control of press rights upholds freedom of the press.

3. When a Danish newspaper printed cartoons of Muhammad in 2005, controversy ensued. Many believe that printing such cartoons upholds press freedom, while others are offended by the images because of religious beliefs, moral opinions, or specific media ethics. English journalist Simon Jenkins opposes the printing of these cartoons, claiming they threaten, rather than strengthen, press freedom. Using his viewpoint as a reference, make an argument for or against printing the Muhammad cartoons.

Chapter 2: Artistic Expression and Censorship

1. Using examples from the viewpoints in this chapter, identify the different motivations for censoring displays of artistic expression. Do you find any of the arguments for censorship persuasive? Why or why not?

2. You are a council person in a city whose local museum is displaying a controversial work. The council is debating

whether to ban the work. A review in the paper calls the work "shocking." Your friends have mixed reviews, and have called the work "obscene," "brilliant," "inappropriate," and "thought-provoking." What would you do? Does it matter if you consider the work to be art, or if most of the town residents favor keeping the work on display? Use viewpoints from this chapter to support your argument.

Chapter 3: Internet Censorship

1. Internet censoring methods such as filters are imperfect and have been known to block out non-explicit materials and to slow Internet speed. Make an argument for or against filtering Internet content by using examples found in the chapter to support your view. Keep in mind such issues as exploitation, terrorism, Internet speed efficiency, and the interference to educational materials.

Chapter 4: Political Expression

1. During her speech at the World Humanist Congress in Washington D.C., human rights activist Maryam Namazie said, "Saying expression offends is an attempt to restrict it." Using examples from the viewpoints in this chapter, argue for or against Namazie's statement in terms of the importance of political expression.

2. Some acknowledge the murals in Northern Ireland as blurring the line between political and artistic expression. Do you believe the old political murals should be decommissioned and replaced with more positive and neutral images? Using Brendan O'Neill's viewpoint, make a pro and con list for the murals' decommission. Follow with your conclusion.

Organizations to Contact

The editors have compiled the following list of organizations concerned with the issues debated in this book. The descriptions are derived from materials provided by the organizations. All have publications or information available for interested readers. The list was compiled on the date of publication of the present volume; the information provided here may change. Readers need to remember that many organizations take several weeks or longer to respond to inquiries.

African Commission on Human and
Peoples' Rights (ACHPR)
Kairaba Avenue, Banjul
  Gambia
(220) 4392 962 • fax: (220) 4390 764
e-mail: achpr@achpr.org
Web site: www.achpr.org

The African Commission on Human and Peoples' Rights (ACHPR) is an organization of African nations that began in 1986 under the terms of the African Charter on Human and People's Rights. ACHPR works to ensure the human rights, including freedom of expression, of all Africans. ACHPR publishes numerous annual activity and mission reports, which analyze human rights abuses in specific African nations and across the continent. These reports and more are available on ACHPR's Web site.

American Civil Liberties Union (ACLU)
125 Broad Street, 18th Floor, New York, NY   10004
(212) 549-2500
Web site: www.aclu.org

Founded in 1920, the American Civil Liberties Union (ACLU) consists of two separate entities: the ACLU, a group that lobbies for changes to the law, and the ACLU Foundation, a nonprofit entity that educates the public and litigates on behalf of people who have had their civil rights violated. The two entities of the ACLU are dedicated to protecting the rights and liberties granted to American citizens by the U.S. Constitution, including freedom of speech, freedom of the press, freedom of assembly, freedom of religion, and the right to privacy. The ACLU publishes numerous reports, podcasts, blogs, and multimedia presentations on its Web site.

Amnesty International
1 Easton Street, London   WC 1X 0DW
    UK
+44 20 7413 5500 • fax: +44 20 7956 1157
e-mail: info@amnesty.org
Web site: www.amnesty.org

Founded in the United Kingdom in 1961, Amnesty International is a nongovernmental organization that campaigns around the world for the protection and promotion of human rights. Amnesty International works to draw attention to and mobilize public opinion on human rights abuses in order to place international political pressure on the perpetrators of the abuse. Amnesty International frequently publishes news features and reports on global human rights abuses on its Web site.

Article 19
6-8 Amwell Street, London   EC1R 1UQ
    United Kingdom
+44 20 7278 9292 • fax: +44 20 7278 7660
e-mail: info@article19.org
Web site: www.article19.org

Article 19 was founded in the United Kingdom in 1987 to promote freedom of expression and freedom of information around the world. Working with over eighty nongovernmental organizations worldwide, Article 19 researches, lobbies, campaigns, and litigates against laws and policies that censor speech. Article 19 has over two thousand publications available online and hundreds of titles available for purchase in print.

Beacon for Freedom of Expression
Henrik Ibsens Gate 110, Oslo   NO-0255
   Norway
+47 23 27 61 72.
e-mail:beacon@nb.no
Web site: www.beaconforfreedom.org

The Norwegian Forum for Freedom of Expression founded
the Beacon for Freedom of Expression in Norway in 1995,
and the project is currently administered by the National Library of Norway and funded by the Norwegian Ministry of
Culture and Church Affairs. The Beacon for Freedom of Expression maintains a database of books and newspapers, from
around the world, that have been censored in the past decade;
this database may be viewed on its Web site.

Committee to Protect Journalists (CPJ)
330 Seventh Avenue, 11th Floor, New York, NY   10001
(212) 465-1004 • fax: (212) 465-9568
e-mail: info@cpj.org
Web site: www.cpj.org

A group of U.S. journalists founded the nonprofit Committee
to Protect Journalists (CPJ) in 1981 in response to the harassment and danger faced by journalists from authoritarian regimes. The CPJ seeks to promote freedom of the press around
the world by exposing abuse of the press and organizing protests and diplomatic challenges to such abuses. CPJ also monitors safety risks to journalists, including tracking journalist
killings. CPJ publishes the magazine, *Dangerous Assignments*,
and numerous online reports and news stories.

Electronic Frontier Foundation (EFF)
454 Shotwell Street, San Francisco, CA   94110-1914
(415) 436-9333 • fax: (415) 436-9993
e-mail: information@eff.org
Web site: www.eff.org

Founded in the United States in 1990, the Electronic Frontier
Foundation (EFF) is a nonprofit organization dedicated to
preserving freedom of expression, particularly as it relates to

electronic and digital media. EFF achieves its goals through public education, lobbying, and litigation of technology-related civil liberties cases. EFF publishes white papers, news reports, and a blog on its Web site.

Freedom House
1301 Connecticut Avenue NW, Floor 6
Washington, DC 20036
(202) 296-5101 • fax: (202) 293-2840
e-mail: info@freedomhouse.org
Web site: www.freedomhouse.org

Founded in 1941, Freedom House is a nongovernmental organization dedicated to promoting democracy, human rights, and political freedom. Freedom House identifies anti-democratic regimes and works to exert international pressure on those nations that do not promote political freedom or other democratic ideals. Freedom House publishes *Freedom in the World*, an annual report on the level of democratic freedom in each nation.

Human Rights Watch
350 Fifth Avenue, 34th Floor, New York, NY 10118-3299
(212) 290-4700 • fax: (212) 736-1300
e-mail: hrwnyc@hrw.org
Web site: www.hrw.org

Founded in 1978 as Helsinki Watch, Human Rights Watch is a nonprofit organization that promotes human rights, including freedom of expression and freedom of the press. The organization researches and monitors international human rights abuses and advocates on behalf of abuse victims. Human Rights Watch publishes numerous in-depth reports on human rights abuses on its Web site, including its annual *World Report*.

International Freedom of Expression Exchange (IFEX)
555 Richmond Street W, Suite 1101, Toronto, Ontario
M5V 3B1
Canada

(416) 515-9622 • fax: (416) 515-7879
e-mail: ifex@ifex.org
Web site: www.ifex.org/

Founded in Canada in 1992, the International Freedom of Expression Exchange (IFEX) is a network of eighty nonprofit and nongovernmental organizations dedicated to promoting and protecting freedom of expression around the world. IFEX reports on threats to freedom of expression and coordinates efforts among its members to address these threats through increasing public awareness, promoting freedom of expression, facilitating international advocacy, and strengthening international institutions that promote freedom of expression. IFEX publishes *IFEX Digest*, a twice-weekly publication that highlights recent cases involving infringements on freedom of expression.

Reporters Without Borders (RWB)
47 Rue Vivienne, Paris   75002
   France
33 1 44 83 84 84 • fax: 33 1 45 23 11 51
e-mail: rsf@rsf.org
Web site: www.rsf.org

Reporters Without Borders (RWB) is a nongovernmental organization founded in France in 1985 to promote freedom of the press. RWB opposes censorship, defends imprisoned journalists, and works to improve safety for journalists. RWB has published several books of photographs to raise funds, and publishes regular reports on its Web site, including its annual *Press Freedom Index*, which ranks the freedom of the press in every nation.

Bibliography of Books

Anthony Aldgate — *Censorship in Theatre and Cinema.* Edinburgh, UK: Edinburgh University Press, 2005.

Larry Alexander — *Is There a Right of Freedom of Expression?* New York: Cambridge University Press, 2005.

David Allen — *Freeing the First Amendment: Critical Perspectives on Freedom of Expression.* New York: New York University Press, 1995.

Jack Beatson and Yvonne Cripps — *Freedom of Expression and Freedom of Information: Essays in Honour of Sir David Williams.* Oxford: Oxford University Press, 2000.

Kristina Borjesson — *Into the Buzzsaw: Leading Journalists Expose the Myth of a Free Press.* Amherst, NY: Prometheus Books, 2004.

Cathy Byrd and Susan Richmond — *Potentially Harmful: The Art of American Censorship.* Atlanta: Georgia State University, 2006.

Dragos Cucereanu — *Aspects of Regulating Freedom of Expression on the Internet.* Antwerp, Belgium: Intersentia, 2008.

Nancy Day — *Censorship: Or Freedom of Expression?* Minneapolis, MN: Lerner Publishing Group, 2000.

Stanley Fish   *There's No Such Thing as Free Speech: And It's a Good Thing, Too.* New York: Oxford University Press USA, 1994.

Freedom House   *Freedom of the Press 2008: A Global Survey of Media Independence.* Lanham, MD: Rowman & Littlefield, 2008.

Ian C. Friedman   *Freedom of Speech and the Press.* New York: Facts on File, 2005.

Mike Godwin   *Cyber Rights: Defending Free Speech in the Digital Age.* Cambridge, MA: MIT Press, 1998.

Mohammad Hashim Kamali   *Freedom of Expression in Islam.* Cambridge: Islamic Texts Society, 1997.

Song-Man Kim, Ruth Cobb, and Drake Zimmerman   *Enduring the Darkness: A Story of Conscience, Hope, and Triumph: Letters from Kim Song-Man, an Amnesty International Prisoner of Conscience.* Normal, IL: Amnesty International Adoption Group #202, 2002.

Anthony Lewis   *Freedom for the Thought That We Hate: A Biography of the First Amendment.* New York: Basic Books, 2008.

Jairo Lugo   *The Media in Latin America.* Maidenhead: Open University Press, 2008.

James Magee   *Freedom of Expression.* Westport, CT: Greenwood Press, 2002.

Jane Mills *The Money Shot: Cinema, Sin, and Censorship*. Annandale, NSW: Pluto Press Australia, 2001.

Glen Newey, ed. *Freedom of Expression: Counting the Costs*. Cambridge: Cambridge Scholars Publishing, 2007.

Erik Ringmar *A Blogger's Manifesto: Free Speech and Censorship in the Age of the Internet*. London: Anthem Press, 2007.

David L. Robb *Operation Hollywood: How the Pentagon Shapes and Censors the Movies*. Amherst, NY: Prometheus Books, 2004.

Joseph Russomanno *Defending the First: Commentary on the First Amendment Issues and Cases*. Mahwah, NJ: Lawrence Erlbaum Associates, 2005.

Joseph Russomanno *Speaking Our Minds: Conversations with the People Behind Landmark First Amendment Cases*. Mahwah, NJ: Lawrence Erlbaum Associates, 2002.

Joel Simon and Carl Bernstein *Attacks on the Press in 2008: A Worldwide Survey by the Committee to Protect Journalists*. New York: Committee to Protect Journalists, 2009.

Sarah Jane Smith *Children, Cinema, and Censorship: From Dracula to the Dead End Kids*. New York: Palgrave Macmillan, 2005.

Geoffrey R. Stone   *Perilous Times: Free Speech in Wartime from the Sedition Act of 1798 to the War on Terrorism.* New York: W.W. Norton & Company, 2004.

Clyde E. Willis   *Student's Guide to Landmark Congressional Laws on the First Amendment.* Westport, CT: Greenwood Press, 2002.

Justin Wintle   *Perfect Hostage: A Life of Aung San Suu Kyi, Burma's Prisoner of Conscience.* New York: Skyhorse Publishing, 2008.

Minky Worden   *China's Great Leap: The Beijing Games and Olympian Human Rights Challenges.* New York: Seven Stories Press, 2008.

Index

Geographic headings and page numbers in **boldface** refer to viewpoints about that country or region.